T0140948

Markus Helfert
Mouzhi Ge
Howard Duncan (eds.)

Applications and Projects
in Business Informatics

Bibliographic information published by the Deutsche Nationalbibliothek

The Deutsche Nationalbibliothek lists this publication in the Deutsche
Nationalbibliografie; detailed bibliographic data are available
in the Internet at http://dnb.d-nb.de .

ISBN 978-3-8325-3155-3

Logos Verlag Berlin GmbH
Comeniushof, Gubener Str. 47,
10243 Berlin
Tel.: +49 (0)30 42 85 10 90
Fax: +49 (0)30 42 85 10 92
INTERNET: http://www.logos-verlag.de

Business Informatics Group
Dublin City University, Irland
INTERNET: http://big.computing.dcu.ie

Preface

Information and communications technology (ICT) has become increasingly important for organisations in the networked and multicultural economy of the 21st century. It is integral to many social and economic innovations and activities that offer new strategic options for companies. In many aspects of business and management the development of ICT has accelerated the introduction of new methods and processes.

However, despite the continuous supply of new technology, problems remain with the development of technological solutions into usable and effective information systems that solve the business needs of networked organisations. In the continual transformation towards information based networked economies, understanding and developing purely technological solutions is simply not enough. To address challenges of a networked economy it is essential to solve business problems and analyse underlying organisational processes as well as understanding their wider social, economic and cultural implications.

This is the basis of the International Business Informatics Challenge, by which we aim to exchange experiences and findings between students and researchers and to encourage research in the field of Business Informatics and Information Systems. We invited bachelor and master students to submit projects and real-live case studies illustrating how technological solutions were developed and applied for effective information systems to solve the business needs of organisations.

All submitted full papers to the 4th International Business Informatics Challenge were reviewed by an international committee and presented at the International Business Informatics Challenge. These papers were improved and extended by the authors. Ludmila Penicina - student from the Riga Technical University, Latvia - has won the award for best submission with her contribution entitled " The mapping of multidimensional BPMN models to BPEL".

The proceedings provide an indication of the richness of topics in Business Informatics. Papers include themes such as the role of information technology (IT) in business process management, the economical impact of IT investment in organisations, strategic information systems (IS) planning in organisations as well as methods and techniques in IS development. While we feel that the quality and diversity of these papers illustrates opportunities that research in Business Informatics offers, we equally believe that even more students should be encourage and supported to carry out research in Business Informatics. As some examples in this proceedings show, research in collaboration with organisations can be extremely beneficial for both, companies and students.

We would like to thank all those involved in contributing to the success of the first International Business Informatics Challenge, without their intense support this competition and workshop would not be possible. A special thanks to our distinguished keynote speaker Frank Maxwell. We also would like to thank all authors and particular the participants of the Business Informatics Challenge for their papers and personal contributions. Especially, we would like to thank all members of the programme committee for their reviews and valuable feedbacks to the authors. Without their commitment and time the review process would not be possible. In addition, we would like to thank all our sponsoring and supporting organisations.

Dublin City University
May 2012

Markus Helfert
Mouzhi Ge
Howard Duncan

Dublin City University
School of Computing
Business Informatics Group

Friday, 25th September 2009	
9:15 – 9:20	**Registration**
9:20 – 9:30	**Welcome and Opening Session** *Markus Helfert, Howard Duncan*
9:30 – 10:00	**Keynote Presentation** *Frank Maxwell* *Galway-Mayo Institute of Technology, Ireland*
10:00 – 11:00	**Session 1: Business Process Modelling** **Knowledge transfer in enterprise resource planning (ERP) projects** *Erik Nilsson* *Växjö University, Sweden* **Visualising Social Network Data** *Juan Yao* *Dublin City Unversity, Ireland*
11:00 – 11:15	**Coffee Break**
11:15 – 12:45	**Session 2: Security & Privacy, Information Systems Development** **Analysis of implementation of cryptographic algorithms in software development** *Vladislav Nazaruk, Pavel Rusakov* *Riga Technical University, Latvia* **Efficiency evaluation system of steganalysis methods** *Vladimir Ambrosov* *Riga Technical University, Latvia* **Bridging the digital divide: preparing today's youth for tomorrow's society** *Austin Turansky* *Ball State University, U.S.A.*
12:45 – 14:00	**Lunch Break**

14:00-15:30	**Session 3: Social Networks, Knowledge Management**
	The mapping of multidimensional BPMN models to BPEL *Ludmila Penicina* *Riga Technical University, Latvia*
	Employee communication and staffing: increasing efficiency and effectiveness *Chris Kestler, Sean Petty* *Ball State University, U.S.A.*
	An information system design theory for knowledge management systems *Carlos Betancourt* *Växjö University, Sweden*
15:30-15:45	**Coffee Break**
15:45-17:15	**Session 4: IT and IS Management, Staff Workshop**
	Skills management of technical employees *Asif Syed* *Dublin City Unversity, Ireland*
	Achieving flexibility in data center outsourcing at Heidelberger Druckmaschinen AG *Tobias Schäfer and Andreas Nowak* *University of Mannheim, Germany*
	Evaluation of immersive learning projects *Fred Kitchens* *Ball State University, U.S.A.*
	Business informatics: a vibrant career in research and practice *Markus Helfert* *Dublin City University, Ireland*
17:15	**Closing of Workshop: Best Paper Award**

TABLE OF CONTENTS

SUPPORT KNOWLEDGE INTENSIVE WORK WITH SEMANTIC TECHNOLOGIES

Roman Brun, Andreas Martin
School of Business, Institute for Information Systems, University of Applied Sciences
Northwestern Switzerland FHNW, Riggenbachstrasse 16, CH-4600 Olten, Switzerland,
{ roman.brun | andreas.martin }@fhnw.ch

ABSTRACT

This paper introduces an approach to support knowledge intensive work with semantic technologies by semantically enriching processes and then applying reasoning techniques on them. Further, the proposed use cases show the abilities of semantically enriched processes. Finally the paper introduces a possible architecture of a system which facilitates the knowledge intensive work with semantic technologies.

Keywords: Process Reasoning, Demonstrator, NEPOMUK, Knowledge Intensive Work.

INTRODUCTION

Nowadays business process management and workflow management systems become standard to support users in their daily work. The systems and technologies users work with are normally not integrated. But many activities in these processes require additionally to the explicit process and functional knowledge also explicit knowledge stored in other systems as well as implicit knowledge which is often only in heads of people. To address the problem of isolation, our approach is to combine processes (the organizational environment) with a semantic desktop (the personal environment). A semantic desktop gives the users the possibility to store their digital information like, documents, contacts, etc. semantically. This means, the data is accessible and queryable as RDF graph. (Sauermann et. al, 2005) Further on, the elicitation of implicit knowledge is supported by using a semantic desktop through sharing, tagging and retrieval functionalities. In other words: "The Semantic Desktop is an enlarged supplement to the user's memory" (Sauermann et. al, 2005).

Section 2 describes the research in the state of the art. How to integrate a process ontology into a social semantic desktop (e.g. NEPOMUK) is mentioned in section 3. Then, a use case is introduced in section 4 with whose reasoning possibilities are depicted. Challenges of integrating the scenario into the chosen environment are explained in section 5 which also indicates the future work in section 6, before concluding in the last section.

RESEARCH IN STATE OF THE ART

GNOWSIS (Sauermann, 2003) is one of the first reference implementation of a semantic desktop. This approach provides the main functionalities of a semantic desktop. The semantic desktop is defined by (Sauermann et. al 2005) as follows: "A Semantic Desktop is a device in which an individual stores all his/her digital information like documents, multimedia and messages. These are interpreted as Semantic Web resources, each is identified by a Uniform Resource Identifier (URI) and all data is accessible and can be queried as RDF graph. Resources from the web can be stored and authored content can be shared with others. Ontologies allow the user to express personal mental models and form the semantic glue interconnecting information and systems. Applications respect this and store, read and communicate via ontologies and Semantic Web protocols. (Sauermann et. al 2005)"

The NEPOMUK (Tudor et al., 2007) project enhances the semantic desktop approach with social aspects. The aim of the NEPOMUK project was to come up with social semantic desktop including Web 2.0 elements.

NEPOMUK, whose goal is to "empower individual knowledge workers to better exploit their personal information space and to maintain fruitful communication and exchange within social networks across organizational boundaries." (NEPOMUK, 2008) offers a framework which can be accessed, used and enhanced. The major objective of the SUPER (Hepp et al., 2005) project is "to raise Business Process Management (BPM) to the business level, where it belongs, from the IT level where it mostly resides now, which requires that PM is accessible at the level of semantics of business experts." (SUPER, 2009). An outcome of this project is a semantic description of the Business Process Modeling Notation (BPMN) (OMG, 2008), sBPMN.

For proof of concept of the approach, the NEPOMUK framework is utilized to integrate processes, similarly as it has been done with KASIMIR (Grebner, 2008) for tasks. To describe processes, the sBPMN ontology of the SUPER project is used as reference. This work is also related to the MATURE approach (Schmidt, 2005). The approach of this paper can be used to trigger and push the mature process by providing refined and user observed processes.

INTEGRATION OF SEMANTICALLY DESCRIBED PROCESSES INTO THE SOCIAL SEMANTIC DESKTOP

In a process there exist different activities with respect to the degree of automation and complexity. As there are already various approaches and technologies available to support automated activities with few complexity (as e.g. workflow management systems or (BPEL, 2003)), the approach supports the non-automated and knowledge intensive activities (Feldkamp et al., 2007) by using the semantic technology and applying standard reasoning functionalities. As knowledge intensive activities often involve human interaction, they are also already partly support by (BPEL4People, 2007) or (WS-HumanTask, 2007).

The state of the art shows that considerable work has already been done in semantically enriching processes (Hepp et al., 2005) and also in the development of a semantic desktop (Tudor et al., 2007). The approach is to combine these two research fields through integrating semantically described processes into a semantic desktop by using already existing technologies.

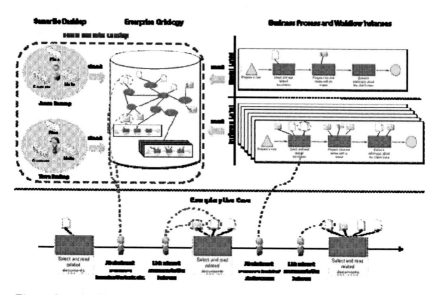

Figure 1:   Architecture overview and exemplary use case

Figure 1 gives an overview over the architecture of the integration approach. The heart of this approach is the enterprise ontology which contains the accessible knowledge of an organisation. This enterprise ontology consists of resources (files, contacts, mails, etc.) shared by the employees. They use the possibility of the (personal) semantic desktop for annotating and sharing files. The enterprise ontology further consists of business process models and instances. This requires the semantic description of these processes and instances and consequently the enhancement of the NEPOMUK ontology as we used it to test our approach.

The exemplary use case (see Figure 1) shows the usage of the proposed approach. Let's assume that Michael has to perform the "Select and read related documents" task (see details in chapter 4 The Use Case (process & instances)). Michael is searching for relevant documents (and other resources) in the enterprise ontology by using the semantic desktop query tools (see chapter 4.3 Reasoning). An example for such a query could be: find documents which are related to a certain topic. If Michael has found some useful and relevant documents, he can decide to link these resources to the actual instance. This gives the possibility to use these resources in further tasks or instances. Thought the integration of process and instances into an enterprise ontology, it is now possible for Michael to retrieve relevant resources in historical process instances which are similar (e.g. have the same topic) to the current case.

The following chapter shows the implementation and usage of semantically described processes and instances in the NEPOMUK framework.

The process ontology and it's integration

For the approach a simple ontology to describe processes (see Figure 2) has been designed. The ontology was designed based on the use case needs and is kept very general and not intended to be exhaustive. Also the predicates do not exist in the indicated ontologies but have rather been named in order to better understand the relationships between the classes. In the following, the used classes and relationships are explained. They have been chosen based on the importance for the work and the reasoning that has been conducted.

A process has relations to tasks (processHasTask), persons (processIsRelatedToPerson), topics (processHasTopic) and artefacts (processHasArtefact); to keep a clear structure there is a distinction between hasProcessArtefact and hasInstanceArtefact in the implementation. A task is related to persons (taskIsRelatedToPerson), artefacts (taskHasArtefact) and to other tasks (hasPredecessorTask, hasSuccessorTask) to describe the order of them. An artefact can be a document, website, person, etc. For the approach documents (artefactIsaDocument) have been considered.

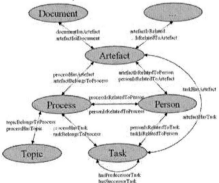

Figure 2:   The process meta-model ontology

Combination of already existing ontologies

The goal was to link existing ontologies together in a way they support the approach and extending it with new classes where needed, but not to create new ones if possible. Figure 3 shows that the class related to processes is taken from the sBPMN ontology (http://www.ip-super.org/ontologies/process/ sbpmn/v2.0), the task from the TMO ontology (http://www.semanticdesktop.org/ontologies/ 2008/05/20/tmo), the class artefact did not exist yet, and any further information element can be taken from the NIE ontology (http://www.semanticdesktop.org/ontologies/2007/01/19/nie).

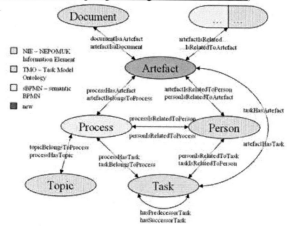

Figure 3: Ontologies combination

THE USE CASE (PROCESS & INSTANCES)

The use case represents a process of career guidance organization. Specially trained Personal Advisers (P.A.s) who are based in schools, colleges, at special access points and so on help (young) people with all sorts of personal issues, including employment and training. The following figure 4 represents a first process in the whole career guidance workflow. It is kept very general and consists of three activities to prepare career guidance. There are two documents related to the first activity. During run-time further documents, topics and further relations might be related to process instances.

For a useful use of NEPOMUK the example test data has been integrated as described in http://dev.nepomuk.semanticdesktop.org/wiki/TestData.

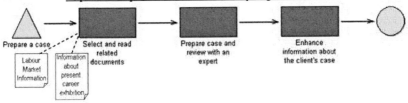

Figure 4: The process "Prepare Career Guidance Case" (PCGC)

First, the Personal Advisor (P.A.) has to select and read documents (Labour Market Information & Information about present career exhibition) which are related to the request. The P.A. might also read additional documents to the given one's and add them if they seem to be relevant for him/her.

The P.A. prepares himself/herself for the case and reviews the preparation with an expert, selected by himself/herself.

As a last step, further information which is relevant for the case is added in order to be optimally prepared for the meeting with the client.

The instances

To go on with the use case, we assume that the following two instances have been executed. During run-time, additional documents have been added to activities and experts for reviewing have been selected as described below.

Instance PCGC1

Topics which are related to the instance:

Plumber

Young woman

Activity: "Select and read related documents"

Additionally added documents in this activity:
- o Information about qualification needs for getting a plumber
- o Statistical reports about young women's profession

Activity: "Prepare case and review with an expert"

The following expert has been selected:
- o Lars Bender

Instance PCGC2

Topics which are related to the instance:

Gardener

Apprenticeship

Activity: "Select and read related documents"

Additionally added documents in this activity:
- Average earnings of gardener in education
- Article "A day in the life of Beni Oudo, gardener"

Activity: "Prepare case and review with an expert"

The following expert has been selected:
- Bernadette Hulgy

Adding the process and instances to NEPOMUK

In order to apply the use case, the process model and the instances must first be added to NEPOMUK. As aforementioned, the existing ontology has been enhanced by creating an appropriate N3-ontology (the process meta-model) an integrating it. To create process models, subclasses of the meta-model and instances of the subclasses have to be created in NEPOMUK.

Unfortunately, in the present NEPOMUK version we used, there is no inheritance possible when using the subClassOf relationship. Therefore the instances have to be built from scratch according to the subclass (the process) they belong to. However, this has no direct negative influence on the reasoning as any information is available.

Reasoning

Let us assume that an instance of another process "Prepare an information brochure for young woman in technical jobs" is running. For an employee mainly working on the creation of information brochures for customers it might be interesting to know who is an expert in the field of young woman working in such typical "male jobs" and contacting him/her. Therefore the employee enters the search terms "young woman male jobs". The system searches for any process instance with such a topic or a similar one. It realizes that an instance of a process with the topic "Plumber" exists. As the topic "Plumber" is a subclass of the topic "male job", this relation can be inferenced. In such a way, the system finds the related expert of the instance and suggests him/her to the employee.

This shows that through ontological stored data, related information can be found which cannot be retrieved in conventional systems. Therefore, employees working in different departments on different processes are easily able to find each other and exchange information. Consider the idea of the semantic desktop where beside process information any other artefact (emails, contacts, bookmarks, etc.) can be integrated. This offers an overall information retrieval by using reasoning techniques. Furthermore, the sharing functionalities of the social semantic desktop framework (NEPOMUK) could give the possibility to access or retrieve the organisational knowledge at a central point (this can be seen as an enterprise ontology storage).

NEPOMUK already offers the possibility to search through ontologically stored information. Let us search for any process instance with the topic "Male job". In the Structured Query Builder the needed classes (subjects and objects) and relationships (predicates) can be chosen and also free text can be entered, including wildcard searches (see Figure 5). These search terms are translated into SPARQL queries which then are executed against the RDF Repository to return the result.

Figure 5:   Structured query for a process with the topic Male Job in NEPOMUK

The result (see Figure 6) is then given and can also be browsed in the side results (see the right hand side of the screenshot).

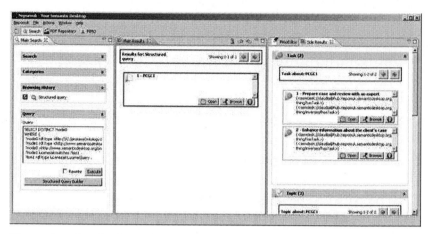

Figure 6:   Result of search for a process with the topic Male Job

Beside this example, further reasoning and uses cases can be thought as for example: Reasoning with much more artefacts like website, person, bookmarks, etc. besides documents), comparing historical cases, reasoning on tags, and so on.

CHALLENGES TO OVERCOME

Level comparison

Regarding (process) modelling, there normally exist the four levels meta^2-model, meta-model, model and instance (Geisler et al., 1998), whereas the later three are relevant for the approach. Figure 7 shows these levels on the left-hand side. In the centre the ontology and on the right-hand side its class- and instance-level is shown. The figure illustrates that it is not possible to distinguish between the metamodel- and the model-level as only the class-level exists.

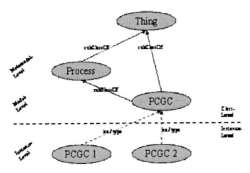

Figure 7: Comparison of standard modelling- and ontology- levels

Process specific needs

A further challenge that has to be mentioned is related to several process specific mannerisms. In a process, in general a task follows after the other. How can that be indicated? Our approach handled this by introducing the predicates hasPredecessorTask and hasSuccessorTask (see Figure 3). Next would be to handle branching or parallelism in a process. This means that it has be ensured for parallelism that a task can have several predecessors but not all of them must have been performed to continue with the task; for parallelism it has to be checked at a certain point that all predecessor tasks have been executed.

However, there might be more challenges regarding process specific needs when going into further detail of process specific mannerisms, which have not been discovered yet. But it shows that NEPOMUK seems not to offer the best framework for integrating processes. One approach could be to use a semantic desktop and a workflow system in combination (see 0 Vision).

FUTURE WORK

To increase the reasoning possibilities, a next step would be to enhance and complete the process ontology. This would require the acceptance in the community by passing the standard review scenario. The modelling of processes in a tool like WSMO-Studio (Dimitrov et al. 2007) or ATHENE (Hinkelmann et al., 2007) and directly integrating the models into NEPOMUK or any other framework would be a further step.

However, the challenges to overcome (see chapter 5) and the according explanation why NEPOMUK might not be appropriate for our purposes forced not to go on with the approach in NEPOMUK at this time and looking for another framework to further develop the idea of our approach.

Vision

The following screenshot (Figure 8) describes the vision how the interfaces could look like. The "Semantic Workflow Workbench" is divided in two main parts, the "Workbench" and the "Reasoning Widgets" on the right-hand side.

The **Workbench** itself contains the elements process overview, task description, task documents, and further the case element with its sub elements. All these elements are generic and their composition can be defined in model time as well as adapted during runtime.

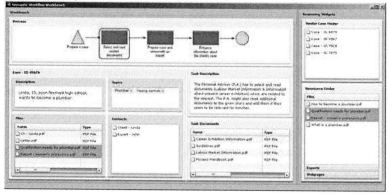

Figure 8:   Semantic Workflow Workbench

The *process* element shows the actual position of the task in the workflow and the *task description* gives instructions about the task. The user has also access to relevant *task documents* like guidelines or a process handbook etc. The system offers the possibility to add additional task documents.

The *case* element consists of several sub elements which will be filled with information at runtime (given by the instance the user is currently working on). The *description* shows the actual case information. The *topic field* contains the relevant topics for the case. When entering a new topic, the field suggest already known topics. The user can find files related to the actual case in the *files field*. It is also possible to add additional files to the case. The *contacts field* offers information about all relevant contacts for the running instance and has the same features as the files field.

Whereas the information of the case element is filled at runtime, the information for all other elements in the "Workbench" part will be defined at modelling time and can be adapted during runtime.

An interesting feature is the possibility to use **Reasoning Widgets**. As seen in chapter 4.3 (Reasoning), the query creation is not easy. Therefore the paper introduces the usage of reasoning widgets which offer an end-user friendly interface. On widget basically offers one functionality, e.g. similar case finder, similar resource finder, etc. These widgets could be developed by software-engineers (develop the widget GUI, access web services, etc.), knowledge specialists (write SPARQL queries) or power users (use query builder as in described in chapter 4.3) who know the ontology and then added as additional elements. Figure 8 shows two exemplary widgets. The *similar case finder* widget provides a selection of similar cases. It is conceivable to refine the similar case finder for example with a rating. The other exemplary widget *resource finder* shows possible relevant files, experts or web pages related to the topics of the actual case. It is even imaginable, that these widgets could be exchanged over a marketplace or a widget gallery. Such a flexible approach would offer the possibility to have a great range of functionalities.

Figure 9 shows schematically the possible architecture of a system which supports the knowledge intensive work with semantic technologies.

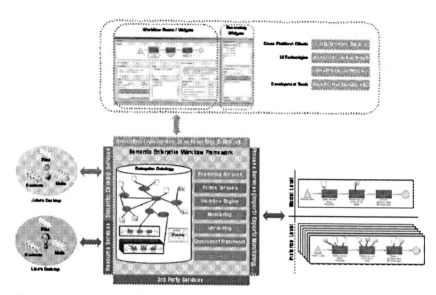

Figure 9:   Possible architecture of enterprise ontology and semantic workflow

CONCLUSION

The approach shows how processes can be integrated into a semantic desktop framework. This means to integrate processes into the overall context of the organisation but also into the personal environment of a person. It allows the direct and easy relation of processes and its activities with any needed artefact as documents emails, contacts, bookmarks, etc. to perform knowledge intensive work.

Additionally, through the semantic description of processes it is possible to apply reasoning in a new way and therefore enhance the support of workers performing a task by offering needed information in an easy and efficient way, especially for non-automated and knowledge-intensive work.

REFERENCES

BEA, Microsoft, IBM, SAP and Siebel Systems (2009). Business Process Execution
    Language for Web Services. Retrieved on
    http://www.ibm.com/developerworks/library/specification/ws-bpel/, 23rd of June,

Active Endpoints (2009), Adobe, BEA, IBM, Oracle and SAP. WS-BPEL Extension for
People (BPEL4People), Version 1.0. Retrieved on
https://www.sdn.sap.com/irj/sdn/go/portal/prtroot/docs/library/uuid/30c6f5b5-ef02-
2a10-c8b5-cc1147f4d58c.

Dimitrov, M.; Simov, A.; Motchev, V.; Konstantinov, M. WSMO Studio (2007), A
Semantic Web Services Modelling Environment for WSMO. Proceeding of ESWC
2007: 749-758.

Feldkamp, D.; Hinkelmann, K.; Thönssen, B. KISS (2007) Knowledge-intensive
Service Support for Agile Process Management. In: M. Hepp, K. Hinkelmann, D.
Karagiannis, R. Klein, N. Stojanovic (eds.): Semantic Business Process and Product
Lifecycle Management. Proceedings of the Workshop SBPM 2007, Innsbruck, April
7, 2007, CEUR Workshop Proceedings, ISSN 1613-0073, online
CEUR-WS.org/Vol-251/.

Geisler, R.; Klar, M.; Pons, C. Dimensions and Dichotomy in Metamodeling. Technical
Report 98-5, Technical University Berlin.

Grebner, O. and Riss, U. Implicit Metadata Generation on the Semantic Desktop Using
Task Management as Example. In: Borgo, S., Lesmo, L. (eds.) Formal Ontologies
Meet Industry. Frontiers in Artificial Intelligence and Applications , Vol. 174 IOS
Press, 33-44.

Hepp, M.; Leymann, F.; Domingue, J.; Wahler, A.; Fensel, D.: Semantic Business
Process Management: A Vision Towards Using Semantic Web Services for Business
Process Management, Proceedings of the IEEE ICEBE 2005, October 18-20, Beijing,
China, pp. 535-540

Hinkelmann, K.; Nikles, S.; Thönssen, B.; von Arx, L. An ontology-based modelling
tool for knowledge intensive e-government services. Corradini, F., Polzonetti, A.
(Eds.): MeTTeG07, pages 43-56.

NEPOMUK Project Summary (2009): Networked Environment for Personal Ontology
based. Management of Unified Knowledge. Retrieved on
http://NEPOMUK.semanticdesktop.org/xwiki/bin/view/Main1/Project+Summary.

Object Management Group (2009). Specification of the Business Process Modeling
Notation (BPMN). Version 1.2. Retrieved on
http://www.omg.org/docs/formal/09-01-03.pdf.

Schmidt, A.(2005). Knowledge Maturing and the Continuity of Context as a Unifying Concept for Knowledge Management and E-Learning. Proceedings of I-Know 2005, Special Track on Integrating Working and Learning.

Sauermann L.. The Gnowsis, Using Semantic Web Technologies to build a Semantic Desktop. Diplomarbeit, Technische Universität Wien.

Sauermann, L., Bernardi, A., & Dengel, A. (2005). Overview and outlook on the semantic desktop. ... 1st Workshop on The Semantic Desktop at the ISWC ....

Groza T.; Handschuh S.; Moeller K.; Grimnes G.; Sauermann L.; Minack E.; Mesnage C.; Jazayeri M.; Reif G.; Gudjonsdottir R. The NEPOMUK Project - On the Way to the Social Semantic Desktop.

SUPER Project (2009) Semantics Utilised for Process Management within and between Enterprises. Retrieved on http://www.ip-super.org/

Active Endpoints (2009), Adobe, BEA, IBM, Oracle and SAP. Web Services Human Task (WS-HumanTask), Version 1.0. Retrieved on https://www.sdn.sap.com/irj/sdn/go/portal/prtroot/docs/library/uuid/a0c9ce4c-ee02-2a10-4b96-cb205464aa02

ACHIEVING FLEXIBILITY IN DATA CENTER OUTSOURCING AT HEIDELBERGER DRUCKMASCHINEN AG

Tobias Schäfer

University of Mannheim, Germany, tobias@bouz.de

Andreas Nowak

University of Mannheim, Germany, derandreasnowak@hotmail.com

Supervisor: Prof. Dr. Jens Dibbern

Institute of Management Information Systems, Department of Information Engineering, University of Bern, Switzerland, jens.dibbern@iwi.unibe.ch

ABSTRACT

Within this business case the outsourcing of server hosting for SAP systems of a leading solution provider for the print media industry is presented. The outsourcing had its seeds in the focus on core competencies and expected cost savings. The circumstances and contracts are described. In the first outsourcing contract a lack of flexibility was identified. In a contract extension modifications were made to achieve flexibility.

BACKGROUND INFORMATION

Company Profile

With a global market share of over 40 percent in the sheetfed offset press market, Heidelberger Druckmaschinen AG (Heidelberg) is the world's leading solution provider for the print media industry with revenue of 3.670 billion Euros (2007/2008). The core business of this technology group covers the whole value-added and process chain in the sheetfed offset sector. All Heidelberg presses destined for the world market are assembled at the Wiesloch-Walldorf site in line with strict quality standards. Standardized presses in small and medium formats and folders for the Chinese market are produced by Heidelberger

Druckmaschinen AG in Qingpu near Shanghai. Heidelberg presses worldwide produce high-quality print products ranging from business cards, brochures, and posters, to packaging and labels in all finishing qualities.

All over the world, the name Heidelberg is synonymous with closeness to the customer, excellence, and trustworthiness from a company that fits based on "HEI Performance" and "HEI Value". Heidelberger Druckmaschinen AG develops and produces precision printing presses, units for imaging printing plates, postpress equipment, and software for integrating all the print shop processes. It also provides general and consulting services ranging from spare parts and consumables to the sale of remarketed equipment, and training at the Print Media Academy.

Based in Heidelberg, Germany, with sites in six countries and around 250 sales offices across the globe, the company supports over 200,000 customers worldwide in the OECD industrial regions and in growth markets such as Asia and Eastern Europe. Its export share is over 80 percent.

At March 31, 2008, the Heidelberg Group had a workforce of 19,596 worldwide. Most of the new appointments were in the field of production and global sales.

Business Strategy

Heidelberg's top priority is to sustainably increase its corporate value. The core expertise lies in the sheetfed offset printing process, including prepress and finishing processes as well. The goal is to be the worldwide preferred partner for sheetfed offset print shops of various sizes and strategic alignments, providing them with everything they need from a single source in order to be sustainably successful in the market.

Heidelberger Druckmaschinen AG offers their customers the highest level of both production and investment security, thereby supporting them in their business success with the industry's most dense service and sales network and highly qualified employees. Additionally, the digital networking of every step of the printing process makes it possible for their customers to optimize their potential in production and management significantly. Heidelberg's comprehensive consulting and service offerings for customers throughout the world include financing and specialized training services.

The print media industry in the industrialized countries is characterized by considerable vigor. The needs of final customers are on the rise, print runs are falling, delivery times are shortened and greater individualization of products and enhanced services are in demand. Heidelberger Druckmaschinen AG also takes the future requirements of their customers into account in their developments and overall offerings. Their solutions ensure maximum performances in terms of print quality, speed, and reliability. Since these solutions considerably reduce the production costs of print shops, they provide an incentive to invest in slack order times as well.

Heidelberger Druckmaschinen AG intends to further increase their business volume in the emerging markets. They offer high quality standard printing presses with a low level of automation especially for the many emerging smaller commercial printing establishments in these markets, thereby laying the cornerstone for long-term customer relationships. They intend to expand their business in the emerging markets, especially in China. Heidelberger Druckmaschinen AG is the first and, so far, the only European printing press manufacturer to establish its own local manufacturing facility. They assemble small and medium-format sheetfed offset printing presses and folders that are especially tailored to the particular needs of print shops in the Chinese market. They are vigorously expanding the share of local procurement. Expanding both production and purchasing in the non-euro zone serves to reduce the influence of exchange rate developments on Heidelberg's profit situation.

Business developments in the print media industry, in particular the advertising market, are dependent on the global economic situation. Heidelberger Druckmaschinen AG is consequently strengthening the business units that serve to reduce their dependency on cyclical fluctuations. These include Heidelberg Services, the consumables business, and packaging printing in particular. In addition, they are continuing to improve the cost structure of the Group on an ongoing basis. Services are becoming increasingly important for the business success of print shops around the globe. Heidelberg's innovative services, such as individually tailored service contracts as well as Internet-based remote services help their customers to considerably reduce the costs of their printing presses over their entire life cycle and prevent equipment failure. Heidelberger Druckmaschinen AG offers the quickest parts service in the industry, as well as management advice, support in financing questions, training offerings for the print industry and used printing presses of tested quality. Moreover, they market a broad range of consumables under the "Saphira" brand name. Saphira products are finely tuned for Heidelberg's systems, guarantee maximum output, and usually surpass industrial environmental protection standards. Because the sales of consumables are largely non-cyclical, Heidelberger Druckmaschinen AG intends to rapidly increase this area of business, including via acquisitions. To a large degree, the packaging printing market is also growing independently of overall business developments. For large format printing, which is an important segment of this market, Heidelberg has developed integrated, wholly networked digital production solutions that offer optimized processes ranging from prepress and printing all the way to the delivery of the printed output.

IT AT HEIDELBERGER DRUCKMASCHINEN AG

Role of IT

At Heidelberger Druckmaschinen AG IT is seen as a support function. So far, there is no significant strategic contribution of IT to the business strategy. Therefore, the target for IT is cost reduction. Standardization of systems, hosting and applications is focused to achieve this goal. Outsourcing was not in scope due to the opinion, "garbage in, garbage out". This means that the quality of a process doesn't increase by outsourcing. As in many European companies, Heidelberg's CIO is subordinated to the CFO.

Heidelberg's IT strategy is supposed to ensure a maximum of efficiency in alignment with the business goals. Optimum service and support to all divisions is supposed to be provided while the cost should be held on a minimum. The IT management learned that they need to be open for innovative solutions.

In 2003 Heidelberger Druckmaschinen AG made a strategic choice as part of a corporate review. They decided to focus on their core business. The focus on standardization leads also to the centralization of the systems like the enterprise resource planning system SAP/R3. SAP/R3 is widely used in the company for example for human resource management and production planning.

2002 to 2004 was financially a challenging period for Heidelberger Druckmaschinen AG. Sales were down and nobody knew when the recession would be over. In 2003 the CIO saw a window of opportunity to reorganize Heidelberg's SAP/R3 database while shutting down the systems for ten days, during Christmas time. In general it is difficult for the IT department to update the systems and install patches because several departments in production heavily agree on a point in time for a required system shutdown. The IT department had very little power to determine a point in time for a shutdown. Therefore the systems were often not up-to-date.

IT Landscape

Heidelberger Druckmaschinen AG has 9000 users of the SAP system. In 1999 the company ran three data centers in Wiesloch (Germany), Atlanta (USA) and Singapore. Centralization of the data centers was supposed to provide better control and management to reduce costs. The data centers in Atlanta and Singapore were shut down and the functions centralized at Wiesloch.

The data center at Wiesloch stretches over 800 m2 and consists of Unix mainframes, Oracle databases and SAP/R3 systems. Storage capacity is round about 50 Terabytes (TB). Performance is measured in SAPS (SAP Application Performance Standard) and amounts to approximate 250.000 SAPS[1].

Also in 1999, Heidelberger Druckmaschinen AG acquired a Swiss Competitor. According to the IT strategy the data center functionalities from the Swiss

---

[1] "The SAP Application Performance Standard (SAPS) is a hardware-independent unit that describes the performance of a system configuration in the SAP environment. It is derived from the Sales and Distribution (SD) Benchmark, where 100 SAPS is defined as 2,000 fully business processed order line items per hour. In technical terms, this throughput is achieved by processing 6,000 dialog steps (screen changes), 2,000 postings per hour in the SD benchmark, or 2,400 SAP transactions.
In the SD benchmark, fully business processed means the full business process of an order line item: creating the order, creating a delivery note for the order, displaying the order, changing the delivery, posting a goods issue, listing orders, and creating an invoice." www.sap.com

Company were supposed to be centralized at Wiesloch. Surprisingly the IT costs of the Swiss company increased due to the centralization. After this observation, Heidelberger Druckmaschinen AG was wondering how the Swiss company had been able to do the IT service cheaper. The reason for the cheaper services was that the Swiss company had outsourced its IT. Therefore the question of outsourcing for Heidelberger Durckmaschinen AG came up.

OUTSOURCING PROJECT

First Contract from 2004 to 2009

Base of Decision-Making

In 2002 Mr. Birkl joined the company and quickly became manager of Heidelberg's data center at Wiesloch. In this position he became responsible for all SAP R/3 systems of Heidelberger Druckmaschinen AG worldwide. He was announced to be responsible for the outsourcing project. Mr. Birkl was supposed to evaluate the benefits of outsourcing the Unix mainframes and the attendant hosting. Hosting includes storage administration, managing processor load, data back-up, monitoring, energy, air-conditioning, security, etc.

Even before Heidelberger Druckmaschinen AG started with its formal offer invitation a first offer was made by TDS Informationstechnologie AG to get an idea about the prices on the market. This offer was much below the current cost. It seemed to be a dumping price. Outsourcing was new to the company so far. They did not have expertise from former outsourcing projects. To ensure the success of the project an expert from Clear View (a specialized consulting company from Frankfurt) was hired as a coach. The expert consulted Mr. Birkl in questions like, which companies should be contacted, what are the phases of the project, how long should each phase take, when should a steering meeting be terminated, when should the board be contacted, etc.

The process of searching an outsourcing partner took about seven months. A call for proposal was made and 12 identified companies were contacted. Some of them missed the deadline. Others had bad reputations, the enterprise was too small, or else they did not meet the service-levels or quality. Those criteria limited the number of companies that met the requirements to five. Therefore the two offers with the lowest price were taken for the final decision, which was handed over to the board and was made "on the golf course". Hewlett-Packard (HP) was chosen as partner and promised 30 percent cost reduction compared to the current situation.

Content of the first Contract and Organizational Changes

In 2004, HP and Heidelberger Druckmaschinen AG agreed to outsource the hosting of the Unix mainframes of the data center at Wiesloch from Heidelberger Druckmaschinen AG to HP for the next five years. Hosting and monitoring were also part of the contract. HP has to create a monthly report of the performance of the systems. A ping-system is used to measure the availability of the systems. The number of helpdesk calls is an additional indicator for Heidelberger Druckmaschinen AG for controlling the service quality. HP had to ensure 99.5% availability of the systems; otherwise there is a penalty, which will stop the next payment.

Since HP began hosting the SAP application, system breakdowns have been reduced. Statistics regarding system availability are recorded automatically. Mr. Birkl only checked these reports in case problems were coming up. In the contract a rise in performance and storage of 20% per year was fixed. This was the expected growth of Heidelberger Druckmaschinen AG's IT demand. HP had to do a technology refresh every one to two years. Heidelberger Druckmaschinen AG provides all licences for SAP R/3, Oracle and Microsoft.

Restructuring:

As a first step, Mr. Birkl handed over all systems and their operations to HP. HP relocated the mainframes from Wiesloch to its huge data center at Böblingen, 115 kilometres away from Wiesloch. It took about four weeks to prepare the mainframes for the transport. Data backups, shutdowns, packaging, and so on were required. The transport itself was managed within two weekends from Friday to Sunday. The transfer included more or less the whole staff, working at the data center. Legal base for the staff handover was § 613a BGB, which requires that the new owner of a company or a part of a company has to take over all rights and obligations concerning employment contracts. Most of these staff is still in the same position at HP as they were at Heidelberger Druckmaschinen AG, others changed jobs within HP. A few people of this IT-staff stayed at Heidelberger Druckmaschinen AG.

Together, HP and Heidelberger Druckmaschinen AG reorganized the processes. HP used its expertise and experience in how to run data centers more efficiently while Heidelberger Druckmaschinen AG used its knowledge of the requirements of its business processes, its SAP applications and its organization of work.

<u>Daily Cooperation</u>:

The daily business at Heidelberg's IT department changed. New organizational structures were designed to ensure good communication and interfaces between Heidelberger Druckmaschinen AG and HP. The former manager of the data center, Mr. Birkl, became governance officer for the operational business and relationship to HP. In this position he had two subordinates who assist him. Due to the high budget of his department for the contract with HP his actions are carefully watched by the CIO.

Biweekly, an Account Review Meeting takes place. This meeting ensures the communication and information exchange that is necessary to run the systems. Responsible people of HP (three people accountable for maintenance, finance, and account management) and Heidelberger Druckmaschinen AG (the governance office) participate in this meeting with an approximate duration of two hours. Main topics are errors and incidences, requests, planning of changes, and capacity adoption.

By turns to the Account Review Meeting biweekly a meeting called SAP Change Advisory Board (SAP CAB) takes place within Heidelberger Druckmaschinen AG. It takes also about two hours. This meeting includes the governance office and all key people and mangers of the software development department. Change requests from several departments are evaluated and approved from a business and a technical viewpoint. This results in particular requests that may have larger effects on the services and may cause risks for running systems. Furthermore they discuss internal developments of SAP applications and related topics.

A SAP Steering Committee takes place on a higher level at Heidelberger Druckmaschinen AG and cares about strategic topics of the worldwide SAP systems. Next to the governance officer CIO and the manager of global infrastructure take part. They make decisions about all SAP systems globally. This includes strategic topics, like release changes. Above this level there is only the board level.

At the end of the contract period:

18 months before the contract was running out and six months before they started in negotiations with HP regarding an extension to the contract, Mr. Birkl setup an additional server which was not part of the data center service of HP. All SAP applications for human resources were transferred from servers maintained by HP to the server by Heidelberger Druckmaschinen AG. During this period they had to pay for their own server and the unused service of HP.

Additionally Mr. Birkl deployed legacy staff of the former data center. He called it "shadow competence". This could allow him to run a data center on his own.

New Basis of Decision Making for Contract Extension

Experiences from Co-Operation with HP due to the first Contract

Due to the reorganization of the processes the process quality improved in terms of speed and availability. Mr. Birkl changed his mind about outsourcing. He kept the saying "garbage in, garbage out" as characterising an outsourcing process since he did not think that bad processes (garbage) could be optimized in co-operation between the outsourcer and the insourcer. But they did so and the outsourcing led to an optimization of processes. This was possible, because HP had core competencies in data center hosting and brought in their experience. Heidelberger Druckmaschinen AG brought in their knowledge of the requirements for their business. Therefore they jointly improved the quality of services.

The early stages were conditioned by resistance to changes and staff turnover by the workforce. The working atmosphere was moody due to the uncertainty of the future. These circumstances didn't knock Mr. Birkl and the board off course of cost reduction by outsourcing. Later they realized that there are much better career options for IT people at HP compared to the small IT department of Heidelberger Druckmaschinen AG. A main reason for the reversal of opinion by the outsourced IT-staff was the higher appreciation of their qualifications due to the role of IT-knowledge at HP – it is a core competence. Another aspect is the role of the works committee because of the hours of work. The IT-staff has to host hardware in a machinery construction company in a time slot when no one needs the IT. These time slots are in the night or at the weekend and not in the regular working time on a construction machinery company. Thus the working committee has to be asked to allow each work effort. At an IT-service company like HP, such time slots are in regular working time so that no working committee has to admit the working effort. Also it helped a lot, that the old employees from Heidelberger Druckmaschinen AG were involved in the establishing of the hosting infrastructure of the SAP application at HP, due to their knowledge of the systems and Heidelberg's requirements.

Another main advantage of the outsourcing was Mr. Birkl's power to accomplish those changes. These opportunities were provided by huge cash flows due to out-sourcing. Mr. Birkl was able to calculate benefits and costs in Euros, which was very convincing. Quality and efficiency of the data center became topics of interest of the board. Due to cash flows the cost transparency significantly increased.

The promised cost reduction of approx. 30 percent per year was achieved. But Heidelberger Druckmaschinen AG realised that their need for IT performance and storage was not growing 20 percent per year. Mr. Birkl expects a growth of approximate six to ten percent per year and this growth might not be linear. But with the current contract there is no flexibility to adapt the IT resources to the requirements. It would be easy to increase the scale of HP's services by paying additional money. But there is no realistic way to reduce the scale of services by reducing the payments. HP did their calculations based on numbers referring to the planned scale. They would decrease their margins by decreasing services. This would not fit to the goal of maximization of profits. A new solution for the growth needed to be found.

Modification for the Content Extension

In 2008 Heidelberger Druckmaschinen AG contacted HP regarding an extension of the contract. Due to the experience of contract results, the technology level of 2008 was frozen at a base level. To increase flexibility, additional performance and storage will be charged as needed based on a change catalogue. Because of the growth expectation, no option of reducing the service below the frozen level was considered.

The change catalogue includes detailed prices for each change or extension of the mainframe services. HP based the prices for the change catalogue on a rough forecast of Heidelberger Druckmaschinen AG and some past experience. Additionally, the cost drivers were identified by having prices for each change. And frequently changes catch one's eye by cash flows. Thus both companies agreed to extend the contract for another five years from 2009 to 2014. After the signing of the new contract, Heidelberger Druckmaschinen AG outsourced the hosting of the SAP human resource application to HP. The rest of the contract was similar to the one from 2004.

FUTURE CHALLENGES

Some new challenges are coming up at Heidelberger Druckmaschinen AG. The business intelligence system runs on SAP, but those systems do not meet all requirements of the business. It's not easy to get new reports and quick checks out of the systems. People need to be well trained and must be confident with formal rules about (in order to?) how to create reports. Other software was tested and seems to be much easier to use for business people. But this software is not part of the SAP systems and additional servers and hosting would be required. It accounts for a significant share of storage of the SAP systems. If they would take the business intelligence application out of SAP they would have high overcapacities of the services provided by HP. In this case they would have to pay twice. These limitations are given by the new contract. The project leader of the business intelligence project said: "The contract with HP is like a guard railing for us. We are not as free in our decisions as we would like to be."

GUIDING QUESTIONS

How is it possible to improve quality while costs are reduced?

Is a re-freezing of the technology level and change catalogue the best solution for achieving flexibility?

BRIDGING THE DIGITAL DIVIDE: PREPARING TODAY'S YOUTH FOR TOMORROW'S SOCIETY

Austin Turansky

Department of Information Systems and Operations Management, Miller College of
Business, Ball State University, Muncie, Indiana, 47306, United States of America,
aaturansky@bsu.edu

ABSTRACT

The author's team conducted a research project for a local educational organization called Motivate Our Minds (M.O.M.). The team researched many peer institutions, learning methods, and technologies in order to solve the technology problem the client was facing. The project was conducted within a two-semester sequence of senior-level classes in Systems Analysis and Design where the student team used the System Development Life Cycle (SDLC) approach to propose the most appropriate solution. The proposed solution included a four year technology plan which was presented and accepted by the client. The M.O.M. organization immediately began to implement this solution based on the recommendations provided by the team.

Key words: Digital Divide, System Development Life Cycle (SDLC), education, electronic classroom, Multiple Criterion Decision Analysis (MCDA)

INTRODUCTION

In parts of the developing world, fewer than 1 in out of 1,000 people have access to a computer. In comparison, the number is nearly 600 out of 1,000 people in developed nations. (Afshar, 2008; Nadler, 2009) This disparity is a major problem facing both developed and developing nations. The digital divide is the term used to describe the gap between people who have and know how to use digital technology; and those who do not have and lack the knowledge needed to use it. Factors such as income, education, location, age, race, ethnic groups, and disabilities are just some of the numerous factors that contribute to the digital divide. (Closing Digital Divides, 2006; Thrush, 2005)

Bridging the digital divide refers to the effort to provide technologically deprived individuals with access to digital technology and the knowledge to use it. One approach to bridging the digital divide is to make technology readily available in public locations including churches, libraries, government facilities, and schools. To ensure maximum benefits and enable positive results, educational instruction must be provided in the plan to bridge the divide. (Feldman, 2009)

Client Profile

Motivate Our Minds (M.O.M) is a not-for-profit learning facility located in a low-income neighborhood in Muncie, Indiana, United States. M.O.M.'s mission is to assist under-served children, ages six through twelve in first grade through eighth grade, with reading, writing, and mathematics education. Most of the children who attend M.O.M. come from families who own little, to no, digital technology, such as a home computer. Inside the facility, there are few working computers, most are outdated, and some children are limited to just fifteen minutes of technology use out of the three hours they are at M.O.M. each Monday through Thursday. Across town and throughout the county, other children have multiple computers, PDAs, and other technological devices readily available. Bridging the digital divide is important to M.O.M. because with limited access to technology children from low-income families tend to fall behind in the skill sets they need in order to succeed in a rapidly growing and advancing digital society. As a child grows older, it becomes more difficult for them to learn the technology skills they need in order to be productive members of a technically advanced society. (Armstrong, 2008)

The M.O.M. facility currently has four classrooms and a computer lab: Grades 1-3, Grades 4-5, Grades 6-8, the Community Alliance to Promote Education (C.A.P.E.) classroom, and a Computer Lab.

- *Grades 1-3 classroom*: There are two non-networked desktop computers in the classroom. The students are limited to fifteen minutes of use per day, resulting in each child using the computer a couple of times per week.

- *Grades 4-5 classroom*: There are three non-networked desktop computers, of which only one is functional. This computer, when functioning properly, is used by students, tutors, or the teacher. The students are only allowed to use it as a reward if they finish all of their homework. There is one DeskJet printer in the classroom. It is used by the students and the teacher to print homework and M.O.M. assignments. The "M.O.M. Assignments" are things that the M.O.M. teachers assign the students to complete while they are at M.O.M. and incorporate concepts such as reading, writing, math, and spelling.

- *Grades 6-8 classroom*: There are two desktop computers, two DeskJet printers, and one copier to support approximately fifteen students on a daily basis. The two desktop computers are both using XP Professional but are not networked together. Students may complete homework and M.O.M. assignments on these two computers. The students are allowed to use the Internet for their assignments or during their daily thirty minutes of free-time. Student Internet usage is visually monitored by teachers to ensure each student is using the computer to do assignments; not to access inappropriate content.

- *Community Alliance to Promote Education (C.A.P.E.) classroom*: The classroom consists of twelve computers and one laser jet printer, all networked together through a 3-com baseline hub. Currently, none of these computers are operating properly. C.A.P.E. is a program that assists remedial students in learning new concepts that M.O.M. has adopted into their curriculum. The students that participate in this program at M.O.M. have been referred by their elementary school teacher due to insufficient grades in their regular school. The computers in this room are loaded with Waterford software. When the computers were working, the Waterford software was used to teach language art skills to children through learning exercises and games. It also incorporated required pre- and post-testing, which evaluates the students' improvement. When the computers failed, the teachers started using printed worksheets to conduct the evaluations.

- *Computer lab*: The lab has sixteen computers networked together, a projector, and a projection screen. The computers were donated by the Oprah Winfrey Foundation in 2004. All of the computers use XP professional and have Internet access. The room is used both as an open lab for students to use, and as an Economics teaching lab. The students that finish their daily homework, daily M.O.M assignments, and behave well are permitted to use the computer lab.

Consulting team profile

The student team working on this project consisted of three students studying Information Systems and Operations Management at Ball State University in Muncie, Indiana, United States. The three team members were enrolled in a two-semester sequence of courses in Systems Analysis and Design, in which they formed a team to consult for M.O.M. The Executive director of M.O.M., Monique Armstrong, asked the team to assist the organization in its pursuit to becoming more efficient and effective concerning the technology-based learning needs of the students by developing a long term technology plan. By following the System Development Lifecycle (SDLC) the team broke the project into a series of SDLC steps. (Dennis, 2006) These steps included Planning, Analysis, Design, Implementation, Maintenance, and a Post Implementation Review. (Alexandrou, 2008; Gido, 2009)

PROBLEM STATEMENT

After extensive research and multiple meetings with Ms. Armstrong, the team formed a problem statement to sum up the technology related issues and symptoms within the organization. The problem is M.O.M.'s technology infrastructure is ill-equipped to teach the skills to enable students to someday become productive members of a digital society. It was determined that by solving the root problem, M.O.M. would be able to help low-income students Bridge the Digital Divide.

PLANNING

A two-semester Work Break-Down Schedule (WBS) was constructed, project rules/standards were established in a team contract, and team building exercises were conducted. (Marakas, 2006; Wysocki, 2000) The risks of implementing a new system at M.O.M. were listed using a six sigma method of assessment called the Risk Priority Number (RPN). RPN is based on the following factors: the likelihood, potential impact, and mediation of a potential risk, or the ability to reconcile a particular threat. With the evaluation of the risks, the team sorted the risks from the smallest to the greatest. A mitigation plan was developed for each risk in order to minimize any potential threats while implementing the new system. (Bass, 2008)

ANALYSIS

The analysis phase began with three meetings for information gathering purposes; an initial interview with the client, a tour of the M.O.M. facilities, and a meeting to interview students and faculty. After gathering information from the meetings and in depth online research, a feasibility analysis was conducted; including a technological, operational, and economic analysis. As-is and future processes at M.O.M. were mapped. These process maps assisted in the formation of critical system requirements. (Dennis, 2006)

System requirements

In order for M.O.M. to help children become positive future contributors to a digital society, M.O.M.'s new technology infrastructure was needed to address five system requirements: User Friendliness, Secure User Access, Child Protection, Storage, and Speed.

User friendliness

The students, faculty, and volunteers using the system do not have strong technical backgrounds so they require easy-to-use interfaces. In order to successfully integrate into the M.O.M organization, it is required that all system components be simplified and standardized to ensure consistency and ease of use throughout the system.

Secure user access

Secure access is necessary to certain files and drives ensuring that no critical information become unintentionally edited or deleted. The system must give access to only the documents that each individual user needs to do his or her job. Personnel with documented needs will have strict access to information which may include grades, personnel data, and student records. Successful user login will need to provide instant access to software applications, saved files, and the Internet.

Child protection

The students, all of whom are ages six through fourteen years of age, are susceptible to many online dangers. The system must be setup for intruder prevention. Specific websites must be blocked by the system. Internet security and antivirus software must be fully active during system operation to prevent viruses, worms, and other malicious programs.

Storage

Each system component should have sufficient storage capability for both students and employees. Sufficient storage must be available to make all information attainable and the system to remain optimized.

Speed

The new system must be able to access, open, send and receive documents within a reasonable amount of time. In order to achieve this, the network capabilities will need to be fast. The system will need to transition smoothly between programs, documents, and other applications. The system should not lock up, crash, or lag due to lack of bandwidth.

Solution alternatives

Extensive analysis of system requirements and a mapping of M.O.M. As-Is and To-Be processes using data flow diagrams enabled a comparison matrix to be used in order to select the most appropriate method for solving the client's root problem. The matrix that was used in this step was the Multiple Criterion Decision Analysis (MCDA). The method involved a list of decision affecting criterion *weighted* by the client and several alternative solutions *rated* by the consulting team. The total scores for each alternative revealed the most appropriate decision presented in a clear and quantitative format. (Ullman, 2006; Belton & Stewart, 2002) Four alternative solutions were developed, each with different advantages and disadvantages.

Solution design alternatives

The following list describes the four alternatives that were compared within the MCDA matrix. Each alternative had distinct advantages and disadvantages. The alternatives were Off-The-Shelf, Custom Design, Outsourced Development, and Hosted Outsourcing.

- *The Off-The-Shelf solution* involved the purchase of a complete system from a vendor and implementing it as instructed.
- *The Custom Design solution* would use multiple vendor products and integrate them together to form one system.
- *The Outsourced Development solution* would provide specific requirements to a vendor responsible for the creation of a custom system that is compliant with all the organization's needs.
- *The Hosted Outsourcing solution* consisted of purchasing a license to access a product hosted by a particular company. The product is often in the form of a website database which can be accessed through an Internet connection.

Description of criterion

The following list describes the seven criterion used in the comparison of the Solution Design Alternatives within the MCDA matrix. The team presented the criterion to the client who weighed them on a scale from one (lowest desired criteria) to ten (highest desired criteria). Some criteria were broken down into two sub-categories to enable the Weighted Average Method to calculate a more precise score.

- *User Friendliness* referred to the ability of a system to be easily accessible by people with various levels of technology experience and skill. M.O.M. weighted the user friendliness seven out of ten (7).
- *Safety* was broken down into two sub-categories: The first category was *Security* which was the ability of the system to secure all data on the network. Security accounted for 66% of the M.O.M weight. The second category was *Business Continuity/Disaster Recovery* which is the ability of the system to react to and recover from threatening situations. Business Continuity/Disaster Recovery accounted for 34% of the M.O.M. weight. Overall, M.O.M. weighted safety eight out of ten (8).

- *Progressive* was divided into two sub-categories: The first category was the system's ability to be cutting edge at its time of installation. Cutting edge at installation accounted for 67% of the M.O.M. weight. The second category was the system's ability to be flexible throughout the life of the system. The flexibility over time accounted for 33% of the M.O.M. weight. M.O.M weighted Progressive ten out of ten (10).

- *Augmentation* was divided into two sub-categories: The first category was the system's ability to be customizable (most accurately align to system requirements). Customizability accounted for 57% of the M.O.M. weight. The second category was the system's scalability (ability to grow and withstand change without disrupting the processes of the system). Scalability accounted for 43% of the M.O.M. weight. M.O.M. weighted Augmentation eight out of ten (8).

- *Cost* was the total cost of ownership (TCO) of implementing and maintaining the solution. The cost is reverse scored in the MCDA matrix. M.O.M. weighted cost eight out of ten (8).

- *Up-keep* was divided into two sub-categories: The first category was the ability of the system to be easily maintained. Maintenance accounted for 44% of the M.O.M weight. The second category was the Durability of the systems components. Durability accounted for 56% of the M.O.M weight. M.O.M. weighted Up-Keep nine out of ten (9).

Installation was the ease of implementing the system based on current infrastructure, conditions, and personnel. M.O.M weighted Installation two out of ten (2).

Design alternative decision

The team rated each alternative based on the seven criteria. Then, team's ratings and the client's weights were used to develop an MCDA matrix The M.O.M. *weights* were multiplied by each team *rating* to determine a score. The alternative with the highest score was the Custom Design Solution: Ranking 404 points. Table 1: *M.O.M. Solution Alternatives* illustrates the MCDA decision matrix that was developed.

Motivate Our Minds											
	M.O.M. Weighting		Off the Shelf		Custom Design		Outsourcing Development		Hosted Outsourcing		AS-IS	
Criteria	Weight	Rates	Total	Rates	Total	Rates	Total	Rates	Total	Rates	Total
User Friendly	7	6	42	9	63	7	49	6	42	4	28
Safety	8										
Security	66%	8	42	8	42	9	48	7	37	3	16
BC/DR	34%	5	14	8	22	7	19	9	24	1	3
Progressive	10										
Cutting Edge at Installation	67%	7	47	10	67	8	53	6	40	2	13
Flexibility over time	33%	5	17	7	23	3	10	8	27	1	3
Augmentation	8										
Customizable	57%	5	23	8	37	5	23	6	27	3	14
Scalability	43%	7	24	8	27	6	21	9	31	2	7
Low Cost	8	9	72	7	56	1	8	5	40	10	80
Up-Keep	9										
Maintenance	44%	6	24	5	20	3	12	8	32	2	8
Durability	56%	5	25	7	35	7	35	8	41	2	10
Installation	2	7	14	6	13	4	8	9	18	1	2
Total			342.97		**404.13**		285.87		358.39		184

Table 1: M.O.M. Solution Alternatives

DESIGN

After Custom Design was the determined to be the optimal strategy used in developing the system, the next step in the SDLC was to select an operating system to begin the design phase. Included in this phase are the design plans for the operating system, network design, hardware, and software.

OPERATING SYSTEM SELECTION

The Operating System software was determined as the most crucial aspect of the system. After researching three alternative Operating System solutions the team was able to construct a second MCDA matrix to determine the most appropriate Operating System. The operating system software was measured against similar criterion and in a similar manner as the design alternatives.

Three Operating Systems were compared in the MCDA matrix in order to determine the best operating system for M.O.M.: Open Source (freeware), Microsoft, and Linux. Table 2: *M.O.M. Operating System* illustrates the MCDA decision matrix that was developed for selecting the most appropriate operating system.

Motivate Our Minds
Motivate Our Minds Weights and Measures

Criteria	M.O.M. Weighting (Weights)	Open Source		Windows		Linux	
		Rates	Total	Rates	Total	Rates	Total
User Friendly	7	5	35	9	63	7	49
Saftey	6	6	36	8	48	9	54
Progressive	9						
Cutting Edge at Installation	66%	3	17.82	5	29.7	5	29.7
Flexibility over time	33%	2	5.94	3	8.91	3	8.91
Customizable	8	5	40	8	64	6	48
Cost	8						
Up-front	33%	3	7.92	1	2.64	1	2.64
Long-Term	66%	7	36.96	2	10.56	3	15.84
Maintenance	9	6	54	8	72	7	63
Installation	2	8	16	5	10	4	8
Compatibility	6	3	18	10	60	7	42
Total			267.64		**368.81**		321.10

Table 2: M.O.M. Operating System

NETWORK DESIGN

M.O.M. has three important functions it must perform in order to operate. These functions include the tutoring of all students; the Community Alliance to promote Education (C.A.P.E.) program which assists remedial students; and an administrative function. Physical and functional requirements were assessed before developing the network design depicted in Figure 1: *Network Architecture*.

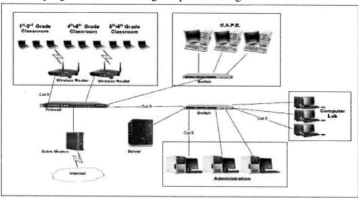

Figure 1: Network Architecture

HARDWARE

In the information gathering stage, M.O.M. expressed the organization's interest in pursuing a learning program called Project Based Learning. Project Based Learning (PBL) is a method that teaches students through a series of team-based projects and activities that require skills from multiple subject matters including math, language, technology, science, and more. It is a program adopted by many high schools (grades, 9-12) in the United States which are commonly referred to as New Tech High Schools. (Pearl, 2009) After the team attended a state wide teleconference on this concept, it was clear that if possible, the new system should assist in the ability to host project based learning.

After extensive research, mini laptops were determined to be most suitable in a project based learning environment. The ideal machines implemented into the M.O.M. facility would have: Windows operating system, wireless capabilities, an 8 GB or larger hard drive, at least 1 GB of RAM (system memory) and multiple USB ports. The decision for the most suitable vendor to support M.O.M.'s hardware requirements was selected through examination of specifications, prices, services and benefits, as well as the vendor's reputation. The decision was made to invest in Dell's Inspiron Mini 9 which was priced at $320.00 per machine. At the time, the Dell Mini 9 had not been released for resale yet, so a prototype of the Mini 9 was acquired from Dell for demonstration to the client, Ms. Armstrong. (Dell, 2009)

Durability and the possibility of theft were issues of concern for the laptops. For security purposes, the team recommended a laptop security cable lock for each laptop to secure them to tables while being used. Teachers will be provided the only keys for locking/unlocking the security cables. Also recommended was a mobile laptop cart to lock up the equipment after hours, and to potentially transport the equipment to other sites which aligned with an initial request from M.O.M. to incorporate a "Mobile Lab". (Products, 2009)

Other hardware included: Super Talent 8 GB flash drives for data storage, Cisco 24-port and 36-port switches, two Linksys wireless routers, a Cisco physical firewall, and Cat 6 networking cable. (Cisco, 2009)

SOFTWARE

After determining the Operating System and specific hardware, a vulnerability assessment was conducted. The vulnerability assessment allowed the team to mitigate each risk through a suitable solution. The two greatest vulnerabilities were child protection and maintenance. (Dennis, 2006)

Child protection Software was deemed necessary for the system to filter everything downloaded from the Internet. Children attending M.O.M. (ages 6-14) should not be exposed to everything on the Internet. The filter would enable blocking of inappropriate searches, custom blocking of specific sites, and the protection of children from online predator threats. An award winning software called Net Nanny was selected as the most appropriate to manage the children's access to the Internet. (NetNanny, 2009)

Maintenance software was recommended to allow the system to remain clean. The team acknowledged that a system functioning in a school setting must have a Business Continuity and Disaster Recovery method for file management considering the number of users who would have access. Software called SteadyState was proposed which functioned by performing backs ups of any and all core operating system files and configuration files, while deleting files that were downloaded or stored to the hard drive during the day. It would restore a standard image to all computers on the network. (SteadyState, 2009)

Other software requirements included an office-type application, and specific software for teaching. Open Office, an open source solution for word processing, spreadsheets, and presentation software was recommended for the Inspiron Mini 9s. Using an open source was suggested as an easy way for M.O.M. to utilize the classroom computers in project based learning without escalating costs. For all administrative computers in the facility, a standardized Microsoft Windows and Office Suite, was recommended. (OpenOffice, 2000)

To determine the required teaching software, an assessment was conducted of the specific teaching functions performed at M.O.M. M.O.M divides its normal daily operations; Tutoring with day school homework, M.O.M assignments (activates assigned by M.O.M teachers), and free time which must include educational substance. A method called E-Learning was researched. E-learning is a method of using online resources to educate. It was decided that using free, on-line E-learning resources would enable more learning opportunities for the students than any single software on the market. (Downes, 2009) The team provided M.O.M. A list of free websites which teach subjects in Math, Science, Language, and more.

IMPLEMENTATION

The fifth step of the S.D.L.C. is Implementation. A four year timeline was developed in order to ensure a smooth implementation and conversion process.

YEAR ONE

The first year of the implementation plan calls for a meeting with the Ball Brothers Foundation, a respected charitable foundation which provides grants to organizations in the local area. The client was advised to share the provided proposal and budget with the foundation in request for a grant. Upon receiving funds vendors will be contacted, equipment will be purchased and Student Interns from Ball State University will be contacted to assist in the installation of the system.

The equipment to be purchased and installed includes Dell Inspiron Mini 9s, wireless routers, software, and freeware for the grade 1-3, grade 4-5, and grade 6-8 classrooms.

Training would need to be administered to fully utilize the hardware and software provided in the system. It was recommended that M.O.M.'s current staff become familiar with the systemcomponents through educational studies at a local university. If however training current staff is indentified as not being cost effective, it was suggested a qualified individual should be hired to handle daily maintenance with the new system.

The acceptable user policy, or AUP, a state-wide accepted policy for public school students regarding Internet usage, will need to be signed. It is a formal agreement between the students and the school, stating what content is acceptable for Internet browsing at school. The AUP is to be signed by the student, the students' parents, and the school teacher. (Cromwell, 2007)

YEAR TWO

In the second year, the current printers in the facility will be recycled and replaced with new ones and the computers in the C.A.P.E. classroom will be replaced.

YEAR THREE

The purchase of new computers for the computer lab was scheduled for the third year of implementation. It is also suggested that M.O.M. apply for an award called the Tech Point Mira Award at this time, which will benefit the organization by being recognized on a state-wide level for innovative use of technology for education. (Stewart, 2009)

YEAR FOUR

During the fourth year it is recommended that new administration computers be purchased and then a scheduled rollover can take place in the fifth year. The approximate cost of implementation is $48,026.74 which is just a fraction of its Net Present Value for 4 years estimated to be $299,655.40. The projected budget for implementation (at current prices) is depicted in Table 3: _Implementation Budge._

Motivate Our Minds									
		Year 1		Year 2		Year 3		Year 4	
	Price	Quanity	Total	Quanity	Total	Quanity	Total	Quanity	Total
Dell Inspiron 9	$519.00	30	$9,570.00						
Super Talent 8 GB Flash Drives	$12.99	50	$649.50						
Cisco 24-port Switch	$179.99	1	$179.99						
Cisco 36-port Switch	$210.00	1	$210.00						
Linksys WRT54G Router	$49.99	2	$99.98						
Cisco ASA 5505-50-BUN-K9 1000	$460.00	1	$460.00						
Net Nanny 6.0 One Year License	$39.99	30	$1,199.70	42	$1,679.58	58	$2,319.42	58	$2,319.42
Security STOP-Locks	$39.37	30	$1,181.10						
Laptop Movable Security Cart	$2,301.05	1	$2,301.05						
Dell Desktop	$700.00			12	$8,400.00	16	$11,200.00	8	$5,600.00
Wireless	$219.00			3	$657.00				
TOTAL PER YEAR			$15,851.32		$10,736.58		$13,519.42		$7,919.42
							GRAND TOTAL		$48,026.74

Table 3: Implementation Budget

POST IMPLIMENTATION REVIEW

After each year of the system implementation M.O.M. has been encouraged to conduct a Post Implementation Review (PIR), which lists a number of identifiers of a successful system implementation. In case the PIR were to indicate the new system integration was a failure,

M.O.M. was provided with an Exit Strategy to ensure a smooth transition back to its original system and state of operations.

CONCLUSION

Bridging the digital divide is an important social issue throughout the world, in both developed and developing nations. It is not an easy task, and cannot be completed overnight. It will take determination, coordination, patience, motivation, flexibility, perseverance, and a positive attitude, among many other characteristics. Efforts to solve this looming problem may begin from top-down or from bottom-up. (Smith, 2008) The M.O.M. organization has embarked on a bottom-up approach, serving the children in their local community. After performing a thorough evaluation of M.O.M.'s organization and business processes, an optimized solution was developed for their particular situation.

By assessing M.O.M.'s current situation, and by following the System Development Lifecycle, a solution was developed that fit the organization's current needs. The resulting plan provides a model blueprint which M.O.M. can follow for the next four years. The plan also provides a baseline which other similar organizations may borrow from to generate their own solutions for their particular situations.

While this model suits M.O.M.'s current needs, any adaptation for other organizations should consider the many factors that went into developing this model. Major factors that contributed to customize the solution for M.O.M. include existing infrastructure, availability of funding, community reputation and support, teacher's technology experience, classroom activities required, age of the students, student's existing technology experience, etc.

In addition to assessing the client's current situation and needs, anybody using this model as a baseline to develop their own, should consider the timing. Technological advancements can change quickly over time. Within the timeframe of one school year, new technology becomes available, creating need to review and update hardware and software requirements before purchase. Although M.O.M. was provided a four-year plan, they were advised to perform an annual post-implementation review before making additional annual purchases.

Implementation of the proposed plan at M.O.M. will assist in bridging the digital divide and providing students the skills to become positive future contributors to digital society. The new system will help build students' desire to attend M.O.M.'s facility, especially among those students who do not have access to technology at home.

The technology being incorporated into M.O.M. will be appealing to not only the students, but also the faculty and staff. The employees and volunteers who work at M.O.M. will have improved resources and technological tools available to help educate the students. Most of the people working at M.O.M. place a high value on the intrinsic rewards they receive from helping students. The new technology will provide enhanced teaching methods for educating the students at M.O.M.

After developing a custom designed solution for M.O.M.; the student team concluded the project in a formal presentation to the client in April 2009. The final deliverable was a complete report, detailing all phases of the project, and step-by-step instructions on how to implement the system, train end-users, maintain the system, and conduct an annual post-implementation review.

In the pursuing months since April, 2009, Ms. Armstrong, Executive Director of M.O.M., has secured funding for the first phase (Year 1) of the implementation, and has begun purchasing hardware and software. Installation is currently scheduled to be complete before the next class term beginning in August, 2009.

By implementing the new technology plan, M.O.M. is creating a learning environment that is more appealing to students and more helpful to the teachers; it will help to bridge the digital divide in the local community.

RECOGNITION

The author would like to recognize Dr. Fred Kitchens; the fellow-teammates of the Motivate Our Minds project, Matt Parisi and Dante Kobek; the Motivate Our Minds organization, especially the Executive Director, Monique Armstrong; Volunteer editors Jack Shepp, and Tim Konopinski. Appreciation is also given to the Information Systems and Operations Management Department, the Miller College of Business, and Ball State University for their support of the Systems Analysis and Design projects and Immersive Learning.

REFERENCES

Afshar, L. "Welcome to Digital Volunteers." Digital Volunteers.Org. 31 October 2008 <http://digitalvolunteers.org/>.

Alexanduro, M. "Systems Development Life Cycle (SDLC)." Marios Alexandrou; Web Project Manager. 12 September 2008 <http://www.mariosalexandrou.com/methodologies/systemsdevelopment-life-cycle.asp>.

Armstrong, M. "About" Motivate Our Minds. 8 September 2008 <http://www.motivateourminds.org/abouthome.html>.

Bass, I. "Failure Mode and Effects Analysis - FMEA" SixSigma First. 18 September 2008 <http://www.sixsigmafirst.com/FMEA.htm>.

Belton, V., & Stewart, T. J. (2002). Multiple Criterion Decision Analysis: An Integrated Approach. Boston: Kluwer Academic Publishers.

Dennis, A., Wixom, B.H., Roth, R.M. Systems Analysis and Design, 3ed. Boston, Mass: Wiley Publishing, 2006.

Choemprayong, S. "Closing Digital Divides: The United States' Policies". Libri, 56, Jan.-Feb. 2006: 201-12.

Cisco Systems, Inc. 12 March 2009 <http://cisco.com/>.

Cromwell, Sharon. "Developing an Acceptable Use Policy." Education World 16 Oct. 2007. 21 July 2009 <http://www.education-world.com/a_curr/curr093.shtml>.

Dell, "Dell - Search - All Dell.com." Search Dell.com. 12 April 2009 <http://search.dell.com/results.aspx?s=gen&c=us&l=en&cs=&k=inspiron+mini+9&cat=all&x=0&y=0>.

Downes, S. "E-learning 2.0" ELearn Magazine: Education and Technology in Perspective. 12 January 2009 <http://www.elearnmag.org/subpage.cfm?article=29-1&section=articles>.

Feldman, S. "A view from Cuyahoga County Public Library" Knight Center Community Connection. 9 July 2009 <http://www.knightcentercommunityconnection.org/tag/digitaldivide/>.

Gido, J., Clements, J.P. Successful Project Management. Mason, Ohio: Cengage Learning, 2009.

Marakas, G. Systems Analysis and Design, 2ed. Boston, Massachusetts: McGraw-Hill, 2006.

EMPLOYEE COMMUNICATION AND STAFFING: INCREASING EFFICIENCY AND EFFECTIVENESS

Chris Kestler, Sean Petty

Department of Information Systems and Operations Management, Miller College of Business, Ball State University, Muncie, Indiana, 47306, United States of America

{cmkestler | smpetty}@bsu.edu

ABSTRACT

Companies are continually attempting to streamline operations and promote lean manufacturing practices. Frito Lay recognized a need to become more of a lean manufacturing facility by improving the Crewing Department. This paper is an overview of a two-semester Systems Analysis and Design project to address the challenge facing Frito Lay.

The first semester consisted of research into the functions and practices at the Frankfort, Indiana Frito Lay plant. The processes of the Crewing Department were studied and analyzed. The second semester, using the System Development Life Cycle, provided a complete design and implementation plan. Frito Lay approved and accepted the proposal in April 2009 and initiated implementation in May 2009.

Keywords: System Development Life Cycle, Scheduling Software, Lean Manufacturing

INTRODUCTION

Companies are continually attempting to improve operations and minimize costs in order to become more profitable. Frito Lay recognized an opportunity to improve operations and minimize costs in the manufacturing facility's Crewing Department. The Crewing Department is responsible for creating, updating, and displaying employee schedules throughout the week. Also, the Crewing Department maintains vacation schedules, time clocks, and receives employee call-off notices. Frito Lay requested an updated approach to completing the Crewing tasks, in addition to saving the company time and money.

Profile of Client

Frito Lay markets, manufactures, and sells a variety of potato chips, corn chips, and other snack foods (Frito Lay, 2009). There are approximately twenty North American plants that produce their variety of snack foods; and they constitute the largest division of PepsiCo. Each manufacturing plant ships the products to distribution centers in the region (Yahoo, 2008). The distribution centers then distribute the products to the customer. Frito Lay has a plant in Frankfort, Indiana where approximately 800 employees produce Doritos chips, Lays chips, Cheetos, and other Frito Lay snack products. Every day, twenty truckloads of potatoes and two railcars containing corn and oil are delivered. These shipments play a key role in production for the plant, and quantities are based on the amount of potatoes and corn available (Necessary, 2008).

Profile of Student Team

The student consulting team was comprised of four senior students pursuing degrees in Information Systems, Operations Management, and Computer Science at Ball State University. The university is located in Muncie, Indiana, United States of America. Ball State University is located an hour and a half drive from the Frito Lay manufacturing facility in Frankfort, Indiana. To fulfill project requirements in a two-semester senior-level course in Systems Analysis and Design, the students acted as an independent consulting team working directly with management at the Frito Lay manufacturing facility. The client approached the student consulting team with a project to increase effectiveness and efficiency with all Crewing tasks at the Frankfort, Indiana facility.

Challenge Statement

In lean manufacturing, business processes must flow together at a steady, consistent pace for tasks to be completed in a timely manner. Each process must communicate with the next in a seamless fashion. There can be no interruptions or slow-downs. If interruptions occur, other business processes are affected resulting in less productivity. This can become costly. One process can single-handedly slow down an operation if it does not have the same seamless, efficient data flow the other processes use (Kanigal, 1997). The interrupted or slower process still functions correctly and provides the required outputs; however, there is no possibility for processes concerning the Crewing Department to communicate and keep up with the other processes in the plant. These inabilities, in turn, affect the speed and accuracy of the tasks that get accomplished throughout the plant. Frito Lay requested a full system analysis and subsequent system design to satisfy the lean-manufacturing demands of the facility and create a system of processes that are efficient, effective, and cost-saving.

ANALYSIS

Research was completed and compiled on the business processes utilized in the Crewing Department to supplement the information and requirements provided by Frito Lay during the initial phase of the project. A set of criteria used to evaluate alternatives was provided to and approved by the client. The three types of alternative solution approaches were: outsourced solution, off-the-shelf solution, and in-house solution. The client provided each criterion a numeric weight based on that criteria's importance to the completion of the project and to the company. After performing research on all criterions for each of the three alternative solution approaches, each criterion was numerically ranked based on the ability of the alternative solution's ability to fulfill the criteria. Multiple Criteria Decision Analysis (MCDA) was performed to determine the best alternative solution approach for Frito Lay (Belton, 2002). Upon determining the most appropriate alternative solution, further research was performed. An MCDA was performed with the original set of criterion plus additional, more specific, criteria to determine the final optimal solution to address Frito Lay's challenge.

Primary Research

An initial meeting was conducted at Frito Lay's plant in Frankfort, Indiana. Employees present from Frito Lay were John Necessary, Ramona Ploof, and

Dave Hendricks. The primary objectives were to further determine Frito Lay's goals for the project and to further establish the system requirements:

0   Requirement 1: System must be accessible by all employees inside and outside the plant; keeping in mind not all employees have home Internet access.

• Requirement 2: Only authorized users should have access to the system.

• Requirement 3: Manual systems can be automated but must be compatible with Microsoft Office applications.

• Requirement 4: System should be standalone and not require access to the existing company intranet.

Monthly status updates were provided to Frito Lay via meetings, emails, or telephone. The client also received updates concerning any changes in the project.

Alternative Solution Approaches

Following thorough research and analysis of the system requirements, three potential alternative methods were investigated to potentially solve the client's challenge:

• Outsourced Solution

• Off-the-Shelf Solution

• In-House Solution

An outsourced solution would rely on the knowledge and experience of an external unit. The external company would be provided with full design specifications by the consultants and/or Frito Lay. An outsourced solution would differentiate itself from a competitor by designing a custom solution for Frito Lay. The advantage of this approach is that the client receives a solution perfectly designed to meet their specific and unique needs. The disadvantages are time and cost to develop.

An off-the-shelf solution is designed to fit a large range of company needs. The manufacturer aims to encompass the largest number of potential buyers as possible by creating the product to be flexible enough to meet many needs. Off-the-shelf solutions typically meet the basic needs with little customization and few additional services. The advantage of this solution is a wide array of services and cost. The disadvantage is the lack of customization and ability to fill niche needs.

An in-house solution is designed by the consultants to fit the varying needs of the client's challenge. This approach involves using components from multiple systems that are not necessarily sold together as a packaged design. The multiple products and solutions are used together to meet all the necessary criteria to solving the challenge. The advantage is the ability to use the best features of multiple products. The disadvantages can be maintenance, cost and complexity of the system.

Following extensive research on available alternative solutions and comparing alternatives with company needs, a Multiple Criterion Decision Analysis (MCDA) matrix was developed (Belton, 2002). Some of the criteria weighed by Frito Lay included: low cost, availability of technical support, ease of use, and access outside the plant. In addition, the consultants weighed each criterion based on its ability to fulfill the requirement. Each weight is multiplied together and a total from all categories is determined. The alternative solution with the highest total score is determined to be the best alternative. The highest-rated alternative should have a considerably higher score than other alternatives to illustrate significant differences in solution advantages. The MCDA revealed that the Off-the-Shelf solution would be most beneficial approach to pursue in order to develop a solution for Frito Lay (Arsham, 2009).

Specific Alternatives

After determining the proper type of solution required for Frito Lay (an Off-the-Shelf solution), the Pugh method of multiple criteria decision analysis was performed on the specific alternatives. This was performed to quantifiably determine the specific alternative that would best fit the needs of Frito Lay. Since Frito Lay's challenge is common among companies, especially in manufacturing, there are many specific alternatives to choose from. The main differences among possible solutions are functionality and the ability to customize the solution to the company's specific needs. After assessing the field of solutions, and conducting a feasibility analysis to weed out many of the competitors, three alternatives remained. An MCDA was used to quantifiably determine the most appropriate solution for the company amongst the following specific alternatives:

- Alternative 1: Celayix Software
- Alternative 2: SchedulePro
- Alternative 3: Time Tracker

Celayix Software is a provider for various licensed management and scheduling solutions (Celayix, 2009). Their software provides many different functionalities such as automatic scheduling, time and attendance tracking, employee record keeping, employee usability, and choices for online and phone accessibility. The employee scheduling software provided by the company is eTime Xpress. It comes in a variety of editions and offers a set of features that allow customization and flexibility to match any industry, including the most complex rules found in manufacturing industries. If the current version of the software does not meet Frito Lay's exact needs, Celayix will customize the software to match the needs of its clients. Celayix also provides many different services such as the entire implementation, training, documentation, and any future technical support. One of the most important features in the software is the ability for Crewing employees to create and modify corporate policies within the software.

SchedulePro is an employee scheduling solution provided by EDP Software (EDP Software 2009). This software is a one-time purchase depending on the number of Crewing employees using the system. There are three different versions available to choose from. Features of the system include automatic scheduling, in-depth reporting capabilities, employee record keeping, and time and attendance tracking. The majority of customers and industries that use the software are in service companies but have the software system capability may be used in manufacturing facilities. If desired, EDP includes full customization of the software within their consulting and integration services. EDP provides services for implementation and training, support, and maintenance on system enhancements.

Time Tracker is an employee scheduling software provided by Asgard Systems Inc (Asgard Systems, 2009). The software is purchased based on licensing agreement for the number of employees using the system. The software is developed to be installed on a LAN with very low hardware requirements. There are no features in the application to provide outside access, but with the proper configurations of utilities like Microsoft Terminal Services, VPN, or Citrix Servers, outside access could be available. The software can be customized to meet the policy requirements of Frito Lay. After the solution is developed, the software is delivered to the client by CD. Frito Lay will be responsible for remaining services including: implementation, training, and technical support. In the future, the company does provide updates to the software as new features become available.

During a meeting with Frito Lay, a second set of criteria was established to rank the effectiveness of each potential solution:

- Criterion 1: Low Initial and Install Cost
- Criterion 2: Low Annual Costs
- Criterion 3: Technical Support after Implementation
- Criterion 4: Timely Maintenance
- Criterion 5: Ease of Use
- Criterion 6: Documentation and Help
- Criterion 7: Access Outside of Plant
- Criterion 8: Scheduling Requirements and Preferences
- Criterion 9: Ease of Implementation and Training

The client assigned numeric weights to each criterion based on its importance to the company. Each criterion was weighted on a scale of 1 to 10; with a weight of 1 being least important and 10 being most important. Each alternative received a numeric ranking based on its ability to satisfy the criteria. The criteria were scored on a scale of 1 to 10; with a score of 1 means that the criterion has a low capacity to satisfy the criteria, while a score of 10 means the criterion has a high capacity to satisfy the criteria. Using MCDA, the weight of each criterion and score for each alternative were multiplied to obtain a rating of its effectiveness in meeting the needs of the client. The scores for each criterion were added to obtain a total rating for each alternative.

Low Initial and Install Cost related to the initial set up of a system. The costs include the purchase of hardware, software, licensing, and documentation and training manuals if not included in purchase price. The costs would also include any recruiting or training for existing and new employees. The highest scorer is Time Tracker (9) due to its very low setup costs. Also ranked on this criterion were SchedulePro (6) and Celayix Software (2).

Low annual costs are determined by the annual maintenance cost of the system. Costs include hardware maintenance, software updates, or any upgrades necessary to keep the system running. The costs also include the ongoing training of employees of Frito Lay, as needed. Annual costs do not just include information technologies. Costs also account for Crewing employee salaries and benefits. The highest scorer was Time Tracker (8) due to its very low annual fees associated with the solution. Also ranked on this criterion were SchedulePro (6) and Celayix Software (2).

Technical support after implementation is the availability of resources to fix a problem that occurs in software and hardware. Types of support include: current in-house IT department, a company IT department at another location, or support straight from the vendor. The highest scorer was Celayix (9) due to many manuals and video support available along with phone and e-mail support. Also ranked on this criterion were SchedulePro (7) and Time Tracker (5).

Timely maintenance is defined by how quickly a problem can be solved by utilizing the company's resources. These resources include the abilities of an IT department, and the efficiency of communication between vendors, third parties, and clients. The highest scorer was a tie between Celayix Software (6) and SchedulePro (6) due to modest levels of responsiveness to system errors. Also ranked on this criterion was Time Tracker (2).

Ease of use involves the difficulty that users encounter when using the system. It includes user interface appeal, conciseness and understanding of functions in the software. The highest scorer was Celayix Software (8) due to a simple user interface design that is easy to learn and customize to meet company needs. Also ranked on this criterion were Time Tracker (7) and SchedulePro (5).

Documentation and help is the number and quality of references that are provided to the end users of the system. Documentation can be in the form of help files, examples, forums and FAQ's, etc. Anything that can provide assistance to help maintain or repair the system is considered in the requirement. The highest scorer was a tie between Celayix Software (9) and SchedulePro (9) due to both alternatives provided many manuals, videos, and training sessions for the client. Also ranked on this criterion was Time Tracker (8).

Access outside the plant is the capability of the solution to provide information outside of the plant to all employees. It refers to the ability to provide access from any location with options including: automated telephone systems, web services, personnel who handle phone calls, etc. The highest scorer was Celayix Software (9) due to the ability to have web and phone access outside the plant for employees. Also ranked on this criterion were SchedulePro (4) and Time Tracker (1).

Scheduling requirements and preferences is defined as having a system where employees are allowed to input their individual preferences for overtime, preferences for leaving early, and preferences for days off for vacation. The highest scorer was Celayix Software (9) due to providing functionality for employees to request days off, request daily scheduling preferences, check schedules, and confirm availability. Also ranked on this criterion were SchedulePro (7) and Time Tracker (6).

Ease of implementation and training deals with the difficulty and complexity in implementing the new system. Implementation includes all installation, configuration, and training in order for the new system to get running properly. The highest scorer was Celayix Software (8) due to provided implementation and training on every area of the solution. Training is available for a predetermined amount of hours, but additional training may be purchased. Also ranked on this criterion were SchedulePro (5) and Time Tracker (2).

The total score for each solution was calculated based on the weights and scores:
- Time Tracker = 279
- SchedulePro = 326
- Celayix Software = 379

The results are shown in Table 1: Specific Alternatives Matrix using MCDA.

System Requirements	Weight	Celayix	SchedulePro	Time Tracker
Low Initial Cost and Install Cost	4	2	6	9
Low Yearly Cost (incl. maintenance)	6	2	6	8
Technical Support After Implementation	9	9	7	5
Timely Maintenance	8	6	6	2
Ease of Use	8	8	5	7
Documentation/Help	2	9	9	8
Access Outside Plant	4	9	4	1
Scheduling Requirements and Preferences	8	9	7	6
Ease of Implementation and Training	5	8	5	2
Totals		**379**	326	279

Table 1: Specific Alternatives Matrix using MCDA

DESIGN

After determining Celayix Software was the best fit for Frito Lay, a system was further configured to meet the original system requirements:

1 The system must be accessible by all employees inside and outside the plant,

1) only authorized users should have access to the system,

2) manual systems can be automated but must be compatible with Microsoft Office applications

3) the system should be standalone and not require access to existing company intranet

In order to fulfill the system requirements, Celayix Software's Web Xpress, eTime Xpress, and Voice Xpress software systems were used.

eTime Xpress is the backbone of the Celayix Software solution. It is the basic software package used by businesses for scheduling purposes. eTime Xpress makes scheduling easy with all the tools a scheduler will need (Celayix, 2009). Some of the features include:

- Zero Conflict Scheduling – Message alerts identify conflicts such as double booked, failed skill requirements, time off, exceeds maximum pay rate, and more.
- Auto Scheduling – Automatically assign employees to assignments based on fill rules such as lowest cost, seniority, etc.
- Overtime Warnings – Define overtime rules and be alerted when a scheduled employee will result in overtime.
- Labor Coverage Controls – Ensure minimum labor coverage per shift period is met.
- Skills/Qualification Matching – Define employee skills / qualifications and match

to assignment requirement.

• Group/Team Scheduling – Define employee groupings and skill requirements and simply schedule the employee group.

Web Xpress is an add-on to eTime Xpress. Web Xpress allows employees to access current schedules, submit time off, and many other scheduling functions from any Internet connection. Features and benefits of Web Xpress include:

2 Schedule Publishing – Once schedules have been prepared and finalized, Schedule Publishing automates the distribution process by allowing employees to view their schedules over the Internet.

• Work Confirmation – Allows employees to accept or decline assignments so that unfilled shifts can be easily identified. Schedulers can then focus on filling declined shifts rather than spending unproductive cycles on shifts that don't require attention.

• Availability and Time Off Requests – Employees simply submit their availability and time-off requests allowing schedulers to quickly assign available staff to open shifts.

Voice Xpress is another add-on to eTime Xpress. Voice Xpress allows the same functionality for employees as seen with Web Xpress. The difference is that instead of availability over the Internet, Voice Xpress allows users the same functionality over the phone. Voice Xpress allows employees without home Internet access to view schedules and submit scheduling information. Features and benefits of Voice Xpress include:

• Alerts – Receive e-mail or text message alerts when attendance problems occur.

• Call Track – Verify call location with block call option.

• Employee Self Service – Publish and confirm schedules

The components of the system will be housed at the Frito Lay plant. The required components include: server, external hard drive, phone line, terminal PCs, workstation PCs, Internet connection, wireless router, and KVM switches. The physical infrastructure of the system can be seen in Diagram 1: Network Diagram.

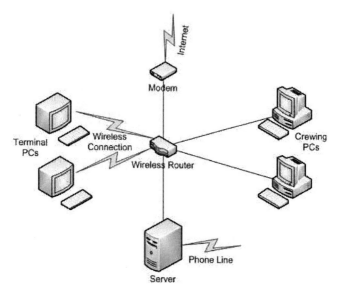

Diagram 1: Network Diagram

Crewing employees will utilize Crewing PCs for scheduling purposes. Crewing PCs will access the eTime Xpress software located on the server. Terminal PCs will connect wirelessly to the router, which is connected to the server. On terminal PCs, employees will be able to access Web Xpress. Web Xpress is also accessible outside the plant due to the Internet connection and modem. Users will access the Voice Xpress program by using a touch-tone phone. The phone line(s) is directly connected to the server.

Server

There is one server for the final system. The server houses the eTime Xpress and Web Xpress software programs. In addition, there is an add-on PCI card for functionality with Voice Xpress. The server does not need to be very powerful to function with eTime Xpress or Web Xpress, however, with the addition of Voice Xpress, the server is recommended to have 4 GB of RAM. A RAID 1 setup will be used with hard drives to decrease chances of data loss due to hardware error. The Dell Precision T3400 was recommended for use as the system's server (Dell 2009).

Crewing and Terminal PCs

The PCs used by Crewing employees and the terminal PCs to be used by plant employees will not need to be powerful. Crewing PCs will access information on the server to run eTime Xpress. Terminal PCs only need an Internet browser, as all information is housed on the server for Web Xpress. The Dell Vostro 220 Mini Tower was recommended for the Crewing PCs and the terminal PCs.

IMPLEMENTATION

With the help of the client and the consultants, Celayix Software employees perform the complete implementation of the system. The consultants purchase the hardware and other equipment. Celayix Software sets up all necessary hardware and software systems and ensures full compatibility.

Consultants initially set up all computer systems and other equipment where necessary. Full functionality amongst systems is insured prior to Celayix Software installation. Celayix Software employees configure the Crewing PCs, terminal PCs, server, and router to ensure eTime Xpress, Web Xpress, and Voice Xpress function properly. Celayix Software employees provide training for Crewing employees and plant employees.

CONCLUSION

The completed 163-page system design, detailing complete analysis, design, and implementation, was presented to Frito Lay in April 2009. The client, John Necessary, approved and accepted the proposal. Frito Lay is currently in the process of reviewing the plan at the corporate level for corporate-wide implementation amongst all Frito Lay plants and warehouses.

ACKNOWLEDGEMENTS

The author would like to acknowledge the collaborations of team members Aaron Lepley, Sean Petty, and Brett Fetzer; and the support of Dr. Fred Kitchens; and John Necessary. Appreciation is also given to the Information Systems and Operations Management Department, the Miller College of Business, and Ball

State University for their support of the Systems Analysis and Design projects and Immersive Learning.

REFERENCES

Arsham, Hossein. (2009), "Tools for Decision Analysis", http://home.ubalt.edu/ntsbarsh/opre640a/partIX.htm

Asgard Software. (2009), "Employee Scheduling Software by Asgard", http://www.asgardsystems.com/

Belton, V. and Stewart, T.J. (2002), "Multiple Criteria Decision Analysis", Kluwer Academic Publishers, Boston

Celayix. (2009), "Employee Scheduling Software and Workforce Scheduling by Celayix", http://www.celayix.com/

Celayix. (2009), "Scheduling Software, Employee Scheduling by Celayix", http://www.celayix.com/p_etimexpress.asp

Dell. (2009), "Dell Laptops, Desktop Computers, Monitors, Printers & PC Accessories", http://www.dell.com

EDP Software. (2009), "Employee Scheduling Software – Schedule Pro", http://www.edpsoftware.com/automatedstaffemployeeschedulingsoftware-Schedule Pro.html

Frito Lay. (2009), "About Us", http://www.fritolay.com/about-us.html

Kanigal, Robert. (1997), "The One Best Way", New York: Penguin

Necessary, John. (2008-09-24), Personal interview, Frankfort, IN

Yahoo. (2008), "Frito-Lay North America Company Profile – Yahoo! Finance", http://biz.yahoo.com/ic/48/48009.html

THE MAPPING OF MULTIDIMENSIONAL BPMN MODELS TO BPEL

Ludmila Penicina

Department of Systems Theory and Design, Riga Technical University Latvia, 1 Kalku, Riga, LV-1658, Latvia

ludmila.penicina@rtu.lv

ABSTRACT

The main goal of the BPMN models is to encourage the communication in the software projects between business and IT representatives. There also exists a standard for process implementation – Business Process Execution Language (BPEL). In the process-oriented software systems projects BPMN becomes an input for the development phase. However in this stage BPMN models are just the description of the workflow in the form of nice drawing. Process-oriented system developers have to refine the given model with implementation details using BPEL to execute it by process engine. BPMN specification offers advanced guidelines for BPMN-BPEL mapping, but these guidelines are useful only if the BPMN process model is constructed from performer dimension – when activities in the swimlanes are organized by a performer. This paper covers the issue of how BPEL process definition changes if the source BPMN model is constructed from another dimension.

Keywords: business process modeling, BPMN, BPEL, multidimensional business process modeling.

INTRODUCTION

The representation of work in the form of business process models can be considered as a method for enterprise systems analysis [1]. In the analysis phase of a software system project business process models encourage the communication between business and IT representatives. This communication helps to ensure that business process models capture business and software requirements identified by domain analysts and accepted by stakeholders. These models become an input for the development phase of the project. However, it has to be taken into consideration that in this stage process models are just description of the work done in the enterprise in the form of nice picture [1]. The main task for the development team is to create executable process definition or code from the given business process model by refining it with implementation details, so that it could be deployed to the process server. The idea of making business process model executable lies at the heart of Business Process Management (BPM) discipline.

To accelerate the adoption of BPM, BPM community has de facto accepted two standards – Business Process Modeling Notation (BPMN) and Business Process Execution Language for Web Services (BPEL) [2]. BPMN provides a graphical notation for business process modeling. It defines a Business Process Diagram (BPD) [4], which is a kind of flowchart made up of elements for modeling business logic (e.g. business rules, event-based choices [1]). Meanwhile, BPEL is an XML based programming language enabling users to create formal descriptions of business process and business interactions in the form of Web services [6]. How these two standards relate? In BPM industry BPMN and BPEL relationships can be described as beneficial symbiosis – BPMN and BPEL can be used without each other, but BPMN model with no translation to BPEL is just a nice looking picture that to system developers makes no sense, but BPEL cannot be used for process analysis in the early phases of project, because it is difficult for business representatives to read and understand it. The best case, in which BPM idea comes true, is when BPMN and BPEL are used in tandem. The scenario for such relationship is as follows. BPMN models are translated to BPEL code, so BPEL can be seen as a refinement for BPMN with implementation details such as data manipulation, Web service bindings and other [1]. Using this scenario the BPMN model becomes a valuable input for development and the main task form the developers of process-oriented systems is to get executable code from BPMN. As BPMN models become the foundation of the development, therefore the following question arises – how to create qualitative business process model?

In this paper qualitative business process model means the model that reveals all the recognizable details of the process flow. Knowing and understanding the details of business processes is important, because this gives the opportunity to identify the bottlenecks and optimize business processes [5]. To reveal all the details of the business process it is necessary to analyze the process from different points of views and within different contexts, i.e., from different dimensions [3]. It means that the process that is represented, e.g., from performer's dimension is hiding in its structure the details about the process from the time dimension. In the result business analyst creates several models – one model of the same process for each dimension [5]. In this paper BPMN is used for representing business process in different dimensions. BPMN swimlanes are used to organize and categorize activities of the process [4]. The idea of representing the process from different dimensions is based on [5]. This paper addresses the question – how the BPEL code of the same business process changes according to the change of the dimension of the process?

The paper is structured as follows. The overview of related works is presented in Section 2. The example of BPEL process definitions generated from BPMN process models in different dimensions is shown in Section 3. Conclusions and future work is described in Section 4.

RELATED WORKS

This section describes the basic challenges and the restrictions of mapping BPMN business process model to the executable BPEL process definition, as well as introduces the idea of multidimensional business process modeling using BPMN.

BPMN mapping to BPEL

BPMN 1.2 specification [4] provides a non-normative mapping from BPMN to BPEL, but the BPMN specification itself is known to be incomplete with respect to capturing all the required information for BPEL. So the mapping presented in the BPMN specification is considered to be insufficient [4]. The specification covers mappings to BPEL that are derived by analyzing the BPMN objects and the relationships between these objects [4]. BPMN specification [4] states that there are known issues with the mapping and the fixes to these issues will be incorporated in a later revision of the specification.

There exist numerous tools that support the execution of BPEL processes [7, 8, 9]. Some of the tools provide even the graphical editors for visualizing processes, however these editors follow the syntax of BPEL, not BPMN [7, 8]. The reason for that is that BPEL as any programming language defines far more syntactic restrictions than BPMN [1]. The elements of BPMN can be connected with each other almost without syntactic limitations – as any flowchart notation, which is naturally unrestricted. This is considered as one of the positive features of BPMN, since in the analysis phase the execution of the process is not the priority, but on the other hand this creates the model that is useless as an input for development. The compromise to this is to determine some restrictions on the source BPMN model, so that it can be translated to BPEL. For example [1] defines that source BPMN business process has to contain no deadlocks or livelocks. The conclusion is that it is possible to represent processes in BPMN that cannot be mapped to BPEL.

The BPMN mapping to BPEL is a challenge not only because of basis of these two standards – BPMN is a graph based notation, BPEL is a structured language based on blocks, but also because these two standards are maintained by different groups – Object Management Group (OMG) is responsible for BPMN, BPEL was created by Advancing Open Standards for the Information Society (OASIS).

Multidimensional business process modeling in BPMN

A business process model is always modeled from a certain perspective of observation – e.g., time, business goals, performers, information and other perspectives [3]. Each perspective of observation may be regarded as a modeling dimension [3] or a combination of modeling dimensions. When observing business process model from certain dimension, the observer is getting all the details only from represented point of view – process activities are organized according to the certain dimension, however business process analyst has to view the process from different dimensions to discover bottlenecks and areas of potential improvement in a process, the most time consuming process activities and the process nodes that could be optimized [5].

In business process modeling phase it is essential for process model to reveal the following basic information about each of the activity performed in the business process:

1. Roles responsible for carrying out each activity in the process
2. Start time/end time of the process and processing time of each activity in the process
3. Documents exchanged within the process (inputs and outputs of each activity),
4. Business rules that control the workflow

Each of above mentioned slots of information can be regarded as business process modeling dimension. According to each of these dimensions a process model can be created and then transformed to another dimension without losing process semantics, using BPMN syntax and revealing information about the process in new context. In this paper only transformation between performer and time dimension is covered. BPMN is a visual language used for business process modeling, and uses a set of graphical elements. BPMN provides four basic categories of elements [4]:

1. Flow objects – events, activities, gateways
2. Connecting objects – sequence flow, message flow, association
3. Swimlanes – pools, lanes
4. Artifacts – data object, group, annotation.

In [5] BPMN is proposed as official multidimensional modeling standard, because BPMN specification [4] describes a pool as the container for the sequence flow between activities, so a pool or a lane can be considered as a container for the flow of activities according to a particular dimension.

How business process dimensions correlate with BPMN basic elements can be found in [5].

GENERATING BPEL FROM BPMN PRIVATE BUSINESS PROCESS IN DIFFERENT DIMENSIONS

There are two alternative options how BPMN business process model can be structured:

1. BPD can contain one pool with several lanes in which activities are organized according to the dimension of the business process, however this approach is not suitable for the B2B situations [4], where BPD has to contain more than one pool to represent the interaction between business partners. In this situation one BPEL process definition is generated.

2. BPD contains several pools (usually in the B2B context [4]), each of the pool may contain additional lanes with activities organized according to the particular dimension, and message flow can cross the boundaries of the pool to initialize the message exchange between parties. In this case BPEL is created for each pool.

This paper focuses only on generating BPEL from BPMN private business process (with one executable pool). The future work will cover the analysis of BPEL generation for B2B situations (collaboration processes), when business process model contains several executable pools and the message flow can cross the boundary of the pool.

In this section are presented the examples of two BPMN business process models – the testing process in a software company and the simplified version of the payment submission process in the university. Both processes are modeled from performer and time dimension and BPEL instructions were generated for each model.

In the case of the testing process the transformation to another dimension was quite simple and required only regrouping of the elements therefore the BPEL code generated from both models is almost equal only differing by the names of the pools. During the transformation of the payment submission process to the time dimension 3 parallel gateways were removed. These elements were necessary in the performer dimension of the process because of BPMN syntactic restriction for modeling parallel activities and synchronization of these activities and were found to be irrelevant in the time dimension model, where all activities are sequential. These updates of the process model in the time dimension resulted in the changes of BPEL instructions. To save the semantics of the process during the transformation only elements that control flow (such as gateways, sequence flow, events) may be changed or removed from model – activities have to stay the same, otherwise the process itself is modified.

Example 1: The testing process

The business process presented in this section defines the order of work for a testing team in the software development company. There are two roles in the testing team – the testing manager and the tester, each participant is responsible for carrying out a particular set of activities.

The BPMN model in the performer dimension

Figure 1 describes the testing process from the performer dimension – all process activities are grouped in the lanes by performer, lanes are organized in one common pool – Testing team. The process model shown in Figure 1 does not reveal any information about time factor in the process – it is not defined when process is initiated and how long does it take for each activity to execute it.

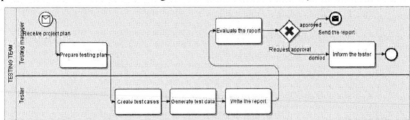

Figure1. Business process according to the performer dimension.

Further in this section the BPEL code generated from BPMN model in the performer dimension is presented (without required namespaces).

```
<bpel:partnerLinks>
   <bpel:partnerLink
name="interfaceAndTESTING_TEAMPlkVar"
partnerLinkType="diag:interfaceAndTESTING_TEAM"
myRole="TESTING_TEAM_for_interface"/>
  </bpel:partnerLinks>
  <bpel:variables>
   <bpel:variable
name="thisReceive_project_planRequestMsg"
```

```
messageType="this:Receive_project_planRequest"/>
 </bpel:variables>
 <bpel:sequence>
  <bpel:receive
partnerLink="interfaceAndTESTING_TEAMPlkVar"
portType="this:Forinterface"
operation="Receive_project_plan"
variable="thisReceive_project_planRequestMsg"
createInstance="yes" bpmn:label="Receive project plan"
bpmn:id="_9h-ooGgXEd65mJjXNiYS5g"></bpel:receive>
  <bpel:empty bpmn:label="Prepare testing plan"
bpmn:id="_Kj2jgGgYEd65mJjXNiYS5g"/>
   <bpel:empty bpmn:label="Create test cases"
bpmn:id="_DRgFUGgaEd65mJjXNiYS5g"/>
   <bpel:empty bpmn:label="Generate test data"
bpmn:id="_kqBwQGgaEd65mJjXNiYS5g"/>
   <bpel:empty bpmn:label="Write the report"
bpmn:id="_8ZGfkGgYEd65mJjXNiYS5g"/>
   <bpel:empty bpmn:label="Evaluate the report"
bpmn:id="_lNthkGgZEd65mJjXNiYS5g"/>
   <bpel:if>
<bpel:condition>
$thisReceive_project_planResponseMsg.body</bpel:condition
>
   <bpel:sequence>
    <bpel:empty bpmn:label="Inform the tester"
bpmn:id="_Yh4SsGgaEd65mJjXNiYS5g"/>
    <bpel:empty bpmn:label="EventEndEmpty"
bpmn:id="_btsucGgaEd65mJjXNiYS5g"/>
   </bpel:sequence>
   <bpel:else>
    <bpel:sequence>
     <bpel:empty bpmn:label="Send the report"
```

```
bpmn:id="_Yx5WkGgYEd65mJjXNiYS5g"/>
    </bpel:sequence>
    </bpel:else>
   </bpel:if>
  </bpel:sequence>
</bpel:process>
```

The BPEL code shown above consists of the following sections [6]:

1. *partnerLinks* – defines the different parties that interact with the business process

2. *variable* – defines the data variables used by the process

3. *sequence* – defines a collection of activities to be performed sequentially

4. *receive* – allows the business process to do a blocking wait for a matching message to arrive

5. *assign* – used to update the values of variables with new data

6. *empty* – allows to insert a "no-op" instruction into a business process

7. *if* – defines condition for exclusive gateway in the process model

8. *else* – defines else condition for exclusive gateway in the process.

The BPMN model according to time dimension

The process model in the Figure 2 reveals important information about the time factor in the process – process activities are organized in the lanes according to time dimension. This model shows how much work is done in the particular period of time.

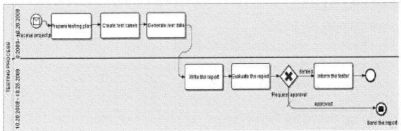

Figure2. Business process model according to the time dimension

Further in this section the BPEL code generated from BPMN model in the time dimension is presented. After the source business process model is transformed to another dimension [5] it still contains one executable pool, however the number of lanes and organization of the process activities in them differs from the initial model. But how transformation to another dimension changes the BPEL code? In this case the semantics of the code after transformation to another dimension is not affected. The only thing that has been changed – is the names of the pool and lanes since they have been changed by the modeler to show the granularity of the time dimension.

```
<bpel:partnerLinks>
  <bpel:partnerLink
name="interfaceAndTESTING_PROCESSPlkVar"
partnerLinkType="diag:interfaceAndTESTING_PROCESS"
myRole="TESTING_PROCESS_for_interface"/>
  </bpel:partnerLinks>
  <bpel:variables>
  <bpel:variable
name="thisReceive_project_planRequestMsg"
messageType="this:Receive_project_planRequest"/>
  </bpel:variables>
  <bpel:sequence>
  <bpel:receive
partnerLink="interfaceAndTESTING_PROCESSPlkVar"
portType="this:Forinterface"
operation="Receive_project_plan"
variable="thisReceive_project_planRequestMsg"
createInstance="yes" bpmn:label="Receive project plan"
bpmn:id="_9h-ooGgXEd65mJjXNiYS5g"></bpel:receive>
    <bpel:empty bpmn:label="Prepare testing plan"
bpmn:id="_Kj2jgGgYEd65mJjXNiYS5g"/>
    <bpel:empty bpmn:label="Create test cases"
bpmn:id="_DRgFUGgaEd65mJjXNiYS5g"/>
    <bpel:empty bpmn:label="Generate test data"
```

```
bpmn:id="_kqBwQGgaEd65mJjXNiYS5g"/>
  <bpel:empty bpmn:label="Write the report"
bpmn:id="_8ZGfkGgYEd65mJjXNiYS5g"/>
  <bpel:empty bpmn:label="Evaluate the report"
bpmn:id="_lNthkGgZEd65mJjXNiYS5g"/>
  <bpel:if>
<bpel:condition>
$thisReceive_project_planResponseMsg.body</bpel:condition>
    <bpel:sequence>
    <bpel:empty bpmn:label="Inform the tester"
bpmn:id="_Yh4SsGgaEd65mJjXNiYS5g"/>
    <bpel:empty bpmn:label="EventEndEmpty"
bpmn:id="_btsucGgaEd65mJjXNiYS5g"/>
    </bpel:sequence>
    <bpel:else>
    <bpel:sequence>
    <bpel:empty bpmn:label="Send the report"
bpmn:id="_Yx5WkGgYEd65mJjXNiYS5g"/>
    </bpel:sequence>
    </bpel:else>
  </bpel:if>
  </bpel:sequence>
</bpel:process>
```

The BPEL code generated from BPMN business process model according to the time dimension consists of the same sections as in the previous example, when business process was presented in the performer dimension. Two BPEL codes are equal – the only thing that is different is the name of the pool in the section *partnerLink*.

Example 2: The payment submission process

The business process presented in this section defines what a student and the secretary of the faculty must do in order to process a payment to the university. There are two process performers – a student and the faculty secretary. The process model contains one executable pool named Payment process and two lanes – one for each of the performer.

3.2.1 The BPMN model in the performer dimension

The business process model shown in Figure 3 contains 3 parallel gateways to provide a correct definition of parallel activities and synchronization construct that makes sure student can pay only when invoice is ready and form is submitted.

The model contains exclusive event-based gateway that assesses the different events the process might receive – the approval of the payment or the timeout – the first one to be received determines which outgoing sequence flow should be used [4].

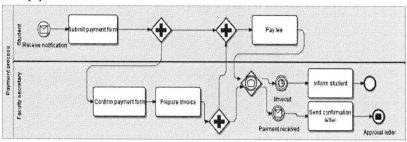

Figure3. Payment submission process model according to the performer dimension

Further in this section the BPEL code generated from BPMN model in the performer dimension is presented.

```
<bpel:partnerLinks>
     <bpel:partnerLink
name="payment_processAndInterfacePlkVar"
partnerLinkType="diag:Payment_processAndInterface"
myRole="Payment_process_for_Interface"/>
  </bpel:partnerLinks>
  <bpel:variables>
     <bpel:variable
name="thisReceive_notificationRequestMsg"
messageType="this:Receive_notificationRequest"/>
  </bpel:variables>
  <bpel:sequence>
     <bpel:receive
partnerLink="payment_processAndInterfacePlkVar"
portType="this:ForInterface"
```

```
operation="Receive_notification"
variable="thisReceive_notificationRequestMsg"
createInstance="yes" bpmn:label="Receive notification"
bpmn:id="_4zBDUJQCEd6l47oaXaxkbA"></bpel:receive>
   <bpel:empty bpmn:label="Submit payment form"
bpmn:id="__M5WgJQCEd6l47oaXaxkbA"/>
   <bpel:flow bpmn:label="GatewayParallel"
bpmn:id="_wMrQ4JQIEd6nV-SCg3JF3w">
      <bpel:sequence>
         <bpel:empty bpmn:label="Pay fee"
bpmn:id="_SxpvkJQDEd6l47oaXaxkbA"/>
      </bpel:sequence>
      <bpel:sequence>
         <bpel:empty bpmn:label=" Confirm payment form"
bpmn:id="_gCVigJQDEd6l47oaXaxkbA"/>
         <bpel:empty bpmn:label="Prepare invoice"
bpmn:id="_J8Wi0JQDEd6l47oaXaxkbA"/>
         <bpel:flow bpmn:label="GatewayParallel"
bpmn:id="_DfI3sJQXEd6nV-SCg3JF3w">
            <bpel:sequence>
               <bpel:empty bpmn:label="Pay fee"
bpmn:id="_SxpvkJQDEd6l47oaXaxkbA"/>
            </bpel:sequence>
            <bpel:empty/>
         </bpel:flow>
      </bpel:sequence>
   </bpel:flow>
   <bpel:pick bpmn:label="GatewayEventBasedExclusive"
bpmn:id="_9f7R0JQXEd68yOaKOPCODQ">
      <bpel:onAlarm bpmn:label="EventIntermediateTimer"
bpmn:id="__6yxwJQXEd68yOaKOPCODQ"> <bpel:for>
$thisEventStartMessageRequest.body</bpel:for>
         <bpel:sequence>
            <bpel:empty bpmn:label="Inform student"
bpmn:id="_Et3fMJQYEd68yOaKOPCODQ"/>
            <bpel:empty bpmn:label="EventEndEmpty"
bpmn:id="_G2vQMJQYEd68yOaKOPCODQ"/>
         </bpel:sequence>
      </bpel:onAlarm>
      <bpel:onMessage
bpmn:label="EventIntermediateMessage"
bpmn:id="_BPTGkJQYEd68yOaKOPCODQ">
         <bpel:sequence>
            <bpel:empty bpmn:label="Send confirmation
letter" bpmn:id="_Ij7x0JQYEd68yOaKOPCODQ"/>
            <bpel:empty bpmn:label="EventEndMessage"
bpmn:id="_LAcQgJQYEd68yOaKOPCODQ"/>
         </bpel:sequence>
      </bpel:onMessage>
```

```
    </bpel:pick>
   </bpel:sequence>
</bpel:process>
```

The generated BPEL instructions shown above consist of the constructs described in section 3.1.1 and additional BPEL constructs [6]:

1. *flow* – allows specifying one or more activities to be performed concurrently

2. *pick* – allows to block and wait for a suitable message to arrive or for a time-out alarm to go off, when one of these triggers occurs, the associated activity is performed and the pick completes

3. *onMessage/onAlarm* – events that *pick* construct processes.

BPMN element *parallel gateway* is mapped to BPEL construct *flow*, element *exclusive event-based gateway* is mapped to BPEL construct *pick* and BPEL constructs *onMessage* and *onAlarm* represent events the *exclusive event-based gateway* might receive.

The BPMN model in the time dimension

The business process model shown in Figure 4 represents the payment submission process according to the time dimension. Its main difference from the model in performer dimension is that all activities are sequential and synchronization construct is unnecessary, during the transformation the parallel gateways were removed from model.

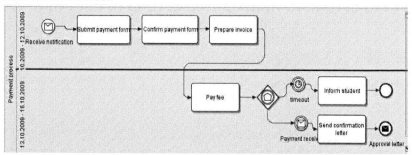

Figure4. Payment submission process model according to the time dimension

Further in this section the BPEL code generated from BPMN model in the time dimension is presented.

```
<bpel:partnerLinks>
```

```
    <bpel:partnerLink
name="payment_processAndInterfacePlkVar"
partnerLinkType="diag:Payment_processAndInterface"
myRole="Payment_process_for_Interface"/>
  </bpel:partnerLinks>
  <bpel:variables>
    <bpel:variable
name="thisReceive_notificationRequestMsg"
messageType="this:Receive_notificationRequest"/>
  </bpel:variables>
  <bpel:sequence>
    <bpel:receive
partnerLink="payment_processAndInterfacePlkVar"
portType="this:ForInterface"
operation="Receive_notification"
variable="thisReceive_notificationRequestMsg"
createInstance="yes" bpmn:label="Receive notification"
bpmn:id="_4zBDUJQCEd6l47oaXaxkbA"></bpel:receive>
    <bpel:empty bpmn:label="Submit payment form"
bpmn:id="__M5WgJQCEd6l47oaXaxkbA"/>
    <bpel:empty bpmn:label=" Confirm payment form"
bpmn:id="_gCVigJQDEd6l47oaXaxkbA"/>
    <bpel:empty bpmn:label="Prepare invoice"
bpmn:id="_J8Wi0JQDEd6l47oaXaxkbA"/>
    <bpel:empty bpmn:label="Pay fee"
bpmn:id="_SxpvkJQDEd6l47oaXaxkbA"/>
    <bpel:pick bpmn:label="GatewayEventBasedExclusive"
bpmn:id="_9f7R0JQXEd68yOaKOPCODQ">
      <bpel:onAlarm bpmn:label="timeout"
bpmn:id="__6yxwJQXEd68yOaKOPCODQ"> <bpel:for>
$thisEventStartMessageRequest.body</bpel:for>
        <bpel:sequence>
          <bpel:empty bpmn:label="Inform student"
```

```
bpmn:id="_Et3fMJQYEd68yOaKOPCODQ"/>
        <bpel:empty bpmn:label="EventEndEmpty"
bpmn:id="_G2vQMJQYEd68yOaKOPCODQ"/>
        </bpel:sequence>
      </bpel:onAlarm>
      <bpel:onMessage bpmn:label="Payment received"
bpmn:id="_BPTGkJQYEd68yOaKOPCODQ">
        <bpel:sequence>
          <bpel:empty bpmn:label="Send confirmation
letter" bpmn:id="_Ij7x0JQYEd68yOaKOPCODQ"/>
          <bpel:empty bpmn:label="Approval letter"
bpmn:id="_LAcQgJQYEd68yOaKOPCODQ"/>
        </bpel:sequence>
      </bpel:onMessage>
    </bpel:pick>
  </bpel:sequence>
</bpel:process>
```

The BPEL code generated from model according to the time dimension does not contain the section <bpel:flow>:

```
<bpel:empty bpmn:label="Submit payment form"
<bpel:empty bpmn:label=" Confirm payment form"
<bpel:empty bpmn:label="Prepare invoice"
<bpel:emptybpmn:label="Pay fee".
```

While BPEL code of the model in performer dimension defines the same activities in the same section using the *flow* construct:

```
<bpel:empty bpmn:label="Submit payment form"
<bpel:flow bpmn:label="GatewayParallel"
 <bpel:sequence>
  <bpel:empty bpmn:label="Pay fee"
 </bpel:sequence>
 <bpel:sequence>
  <bpel:empty bpmn:label=" Confirm payment form"
```

```
<bpel:empty bpmn:label="Prepare invoice"
<bpel:flow bpmn:label="GatewayParallel"
 <bpel:sequence>
  <bpel:empty bpmn:label="Pay fee"
 </bpel:sequence>
 <bpel:empty/>
 </bpel:flow>
 </bpel:sequence>
</bpel:flow>
```

BPEL code generated from time dimension is more readable as it contains less specific BPEL constructs due to removal of the synchronization construct and parallel gateways from BPMN model in time dimension. BPEL instructions from time dimension model can be understandable even for business representatives, however they define the same process presented in Figure 3. The further research must address if synchronization constructs and parallel gateways are always unnecessary in business process model presented in time dimension, or this is more like exception than a rule and applies to the examples presented in this section and similar processes.

CONCLUSIONS AND FUTURE WORK

This paper addresses the issue of generating BPEL code from multidimensional BPMN private business processes. Business processes discussed in this paper describe the testing process in the software company and the payment submission process in the university. For each business process two BPMN models were created – the performer and time dimension model. The source model of each process was presented in performer dimension and then manually transformed to time dimension according to the guidelines presented in [5], however before transformation BPEL instructions were generated from the initial model. Then BPEL code was repeatedly generated from the model in time dimension. The question that paper addresses is how BPEL code of the same process is affected after process is presented in another dimension? To answer the comparison of two BPEL process definitions of each process was carried out – analyzing each line of two BPEL process descriptions.

In the case of the testing process it was concluded that the code obtained from both models was the same, only the names of the pools differed. The explanation for this finding is simple – in the case of the testing process the transformation to another dimension meant only regrouping the elements to different swimlanes, keeping all the relationships between the elements the same. The transformation was so trivial because the model did not contained such specific flow control patterns as merging of the flow threads or parallel activities.

The case of payment submission process model transformation was morecomplicated. It was revealed that in the model according to time dimension synchronization construct and parallel split construct is unnecessary, because all activities from time dimension are sequential. Due to this conclusion 3 parallel gateways were removed from the initial payment submission process. This resulted in the changes of the BPEL instructions – in the BPEL code from time dimension model section *flow* is absent and the sequence of the activities is different. It was also concluded that during the transformations between dimensions only elements that control the flow (gateways, events, sequence flows) may be removed and differ from model to model, but activities have to stay the same, otherwise the process itself is modified.

The future work will address the question about what are the other specific workflow patterns (such as Discriminator, Multiple Merge, Multiple Choice, N out of M Join, Synchronizing Merge) that may be changed or removed during the transformation to time dimension.

In the situations where business process model contains several executable pools (B2B process), BPEL is created for each pool separately. The future work will address the issue of generating BPEL code from collaboration BPMN business process model, which contains message flows that cross the boundaries of the pools and how the transformation of collaboration process to another dimension affects BPEL process definitions of each pool involved in the process and the interactions between these pools.

BPMN and BPEL are important standards in the BPM industry, but the translating BPMN to BPEL is a challenging task. First of all BPEL imposes far more syntactic restrictions that BPMN, it means that the business analyst is not allowed to use certain BPMN constructs in the source model that can lead to deadlocks. Second, as stated in BPMN specification, the guidelines for BPMN mapping to BPEL are not complete and in any case a developer has to be able to read BPEL and alter some sections of BPEL if it is necessary. However BPEL code can be quite hard, unreadable and time consuming. In these situations the question is: what is the added value of the BPEL in the project and is it worth to use it.

ACKNOWLEDGMENTS

Intalio Designer 5.2.0.115 vas used for creating of the BPMN business process models and generating BPEL code presented in this paper. The author acknowledges Professor Dr. sc. ing. Marite Kirikova for valuable comments on the draft of the paper.

REFERENCES

1. Ouyang, C., van der Aalst, Wil M.P., Dumas, Marlon,ter Hofstede, Arthur H.M.: From Business Process Models to Process-oriented Software Systems: The BPMN to BPEL Way. (2006)

2. Matjaz B. J., Kapil P.: Business Process Driven SOA using BPMN and BPEL, Packt Publishing, (2008)

3. Kirikova M., Businska L., Penicina L.: Multidimensional Business Process Modeling. In: The 7th International Conference on Perspective in Business Informatics Research (BIR 2008), pp. 196-210 (2008)

4. Business Process Modeling Notation (BPMN) Specification, http://www.bpmn.org/

5. Pe icina L.: The Approach of Transformation between Business ņ Process Dimensions in BPMN Modeling Tool. In: The 15th International Conference on Information and Software Technologies (IT 2009), pp.72-81. lpp (2009)

6. Web Services Business Process Execution Language Version 2.0 Specification, http://www.oasis-open.org/committees/download.php/10347

7. Oracle BPEL Process Manager, ww.oracle.com/technology/bpel

8. Microsoft BizTalk Server 2004, www.microsoft.com/BizTalk

9. Intalio|BPMS 5.2, http://community.intalio.com/

ANALYSIS OF IMPLEMENTATION OF CRYPTOGRAPHIC ALGORITHMS IN SOFTWARE DEVELOPMENT

Vladislav Nazaruk, Pavel Rusakov

Faculty of Computer Science and Information Technology, Riga Technical University, Riga, Latvia

{Vladislavs.Nazaruks | Pavels.Rusakovs }@rtu.lv

ABSTRACT

The goal of the paper is to analyse common problems of implementation of cryptographic algorithms, as well as to discuss some possibilities of implementing cryptographic algorithms in software development. In the paper, there are defined possible vulnerabilities in an implementation of cryptographic algorithms on a computer, and errors which are the causes of these vulnerabilities are classified. There are given general recommendations, how to escape from possible vulnerabilities. There is also considered implementation of cryptographic methods in software development by using software libraries and frameworks. Several widespread software frameworks which provide cryptographic functionality are compared with each other by several criteria (including the speed of execution of cryptographic algorithms). The goal of this comparison is to construct some guidelines which will help select a feasible solution for implementing a cryptographic functionality in software. Finally, there are discussed some general possibilities of maximising the speed of execution of cryptographic algorithms.

Keywords: cryptographic algorithms, vulnerabilities, software libraries, execution speed

INTRODUCTION

People's life is impossible without communication. In some cases, communication must be protected in a certain manner. In this situation, cryptography — a study and practice of protecting the information — is often used. The goal of this paper is to discuss cryptography in the context of its implementation in software development, emphasising possible errors and vulnerabilities in an implementation of cryptographic algorithms, usage of cryptographic frameworks and libraries, as well as the speed of execution of implemented cryptographic algorithms. The material of this paper is based on the results obtained in the development of the author's master's thesis (see also (Nazaruks 2009)).

In the beginning of the paper, there is given a brief overview of methods for providing information security. Further in the paper, there are defined possible vulnerabilities in an implementation of cryptographic algorithms on a computer, and errors which are the causes of these vulnerabilities are classified. There is also considered implementation of cryptographic methods in software development by using software frameworks. Several major software frameworks which provide cryptographic functionality are compared with each other by several criteria. The goal of this comparison is to construct some guidelines which will help select a feasible solution for implementing a cryptographic functionality in software. Finally, there are discussed some general possibilities of maximising the speed of execution of cryptographic algorithms. At the end of the paper, the conclusions about the work are given.

Results concerning the speed of an implementation of cryptographic algorithms are based on practical experiments — by the authors, there were written and utilised several computer programs for measuring a time of running the specific cryptographic algorithms implemented in some widespread cryptographic frameworks. The methodology used for measuring a speed of execution of cryptographic algorithms is discussed further in this paper.

BASIC CONCEPTS OF CRYPTOGRAPHY

Cryptography is a science which investigates methods of protecting information. A *protection of information* is an activity (or a set of activities) for providing *security of the information*; in its turn, *information security* is such a property of the information environment, which implies the presence of at least one of the following attributes (factors) of the information (depending on the requirements) (Schneier 1996):

0   confidentiality — a possibility to access the information only by its sender and address(-es);

● integrity — an ability of the receiver of the information to discover the fact of modification of the information (if any) by third parties (after the information has been sent by its sender);

● authenticity — an ability for the receiver of the information to determine the real sender of the information.

Cryptography together with *cryptanalysis* — a study of identifying and exploiting flaws in the methods of the information protection — forms a joint science called *cryptology* (which sometimes is also called cryptography).

There exist a lot of different algorithms — cryptographic algorithms, the use of which can ensure the fulfilment of specific factors of information security. All cryptographic algorithms provisionally can be divided into the following two main classes: cryptographic primitives and cryptographic protocols. *Cryptographic primitives* can be defined as algorithms which describe atomic mathematical transformations with specific properties (these properties, in their turn, determine a class of cryptographic primitive). *Cryptographic protocols* mainly describe the *logic* of using cryptographic primitives, in order to realise specific factors of information security. Thus, cryptographic protocols are meta-algorithms which in their work use cryptographic primitives.

Depending on the properties of transformation implemented by a specific cryptographic primitive, these primitives are divided in the following main classes:

● ciphers:
   ○ symmetric ciphers (*or* private-key ciphers):
      ▪ block ciphers;

- ■   stream ciphers;
- ○   asymmetric ciphers (*or* public-key ciphers);
- one-way (*or* cryptographic) hash-functions;
- message authentication codes (MAC);
- digital signature algorithms.

In this paper, the emphasis is on cryptographic *primitives*, and particularly on the *mostly-used* primitives: symmetric ciphers and hash-functions.

Information security factors which are fulfilled by each class of cryptographic primitives are shown in table 1. The names of most widespread algorithms from each class of cryptographic primitives are shown in table 2.

Class of cryptographic primitives	Information security factor:		
	confidentiality	integrity	authenticity
ciphers	+		
one-way hash-functions		+	
message authentication codes		+	+
digital signature algorithms		+	+

Table 1. Information security factors fulfilled by a specific class of cryptographic primitives

Class of cryptographic primitives	Algorithm samples
ciphers:	
— symmetric:	
— block	AES (or Rijndael), RC2, Triple-DES, Blowfish, RC6, Twofish, Serpent, IDEA, RC5, DES, GOST
— stream	Salsa20, Panama, RC4 (or ARC4), SEAL 3.0, WAKE
— asymmetric	RSA, ElGamal
one-way hash-functions	SHA-1, SHA-2, Tiger, Whirlpool, RIPEMD-160, MD2, MD4, MD5
message authentication codes	VMAC, HMAC, CMAC
digital signature algorithms	DSA, GOST R 34.10-94

Table 2. Most widespread algorithms from each class of cryptographic primitives

VULNERABILITIES IN IMPLEMENTATION OF INFORMATION PROTECTION METHODS

When creating or implementing cryptographic methods, it is very hard to prove that the method or its implementation is resistant to cryptanalysis. If people who created a specific cryptographic method, and people who tested it for a resistance have not found vulnerabilities in it (i. e., in its theoretical model or its implementation), then this does not mean that the method is fully resistant to cryptanalysis — even if the manpower used for checking the method was very large. The situations when well-known, widespread cryptographic algorithms which appeared to be secure for a long period of time are successfully attacked, are common enough (see (Black et al. 2006) and (Stevens et al. 2007) for the illustration of attacking the MD5 hash-function).

Vulnerabilities can arise in the entire life cycle of a cryptographic method: during creation of its mathematical model (design errors), during implementation of the cryptographic *primitives* on a computer, during implementation of the cryptographic *protocol* (errors of usage of the cryptographic functions), and, finally, during the usage of the implemented system. Further, there are discussed vulnerabilities in a design and an implementation of cryptographic methods.

Factors which can raise vulnerabilities in an implementation of information protection methods are classified by authors of the paper in the following way:
- errors in selecting a proper information protection algorithm:
  o   errors in selecting a proper class of an information protection algorithm;
  o   errors in designing cryptographic algorithms;
- errors in implementing cryptographic algorithms;
- usage of cryptographic algorithms in an improper way;
- unaccounted specific features of the external environment.

These factors are considered further in this chapter.

Errors in selecting a proper information protection algorithm

Errors in selecting a proper class of an information protection algorithm

The selection of improper class of an information protection algorithm can lead to a violation of the security of an information system. In the information system, there can be used methods of information protection which constraint only an *access* to the secure information, but does not ensure a *hiding* of that information; or in the information system, information protection methods there can be not used at all. In these cases, in order to maximise the information security level, and to prevent a possibility for unauthorised people to get to the secure information by taking the software in, one should use *cryptographic* algorithms.

By using cryptographic algorithms, many necessary actions (e. g., checking the correspondence of an entered password to the original) can be implemented either totally without storing a secure information (e. g., instead of passwords, storing their hash-values), or without storing a secure information in an open way — but in a modified *(protected)* way.

Errors in designing cryptographic algorithms

By far not every invented cryptographic algorithm (including cryptographic protocols) is reasonably secure. To become to a certain degree accepted by a public, an algorithm shall sustain after many attempts of breaking it during a sufficient period of time (at least several months, and if there is enough interest to it from cryptanalysis professionals).

It is needless to say that most of home-made cryptographic algorithms are very exposed to breaking. Many of such algorithms are created without a proper knowledge of mathematics, and without even trying to analyse and break them. Some of newly-invented algorithms are created "from zero", but some are modifications of popular cryptographic algorithms. However, even a little modification of a highly secure cryptographic algorithm can reduce almost to zero all advantages of the primitive (original) algorithm. In fact, even slightly modifying algorithm gives algorithm with different outputs, and thus a different algorithm, which, in order to be proven to be secure, needs to be carefully examined. For example, a modification of one of the efficient group key distribution technique — the subset difference (SD) method — has been showed as insecure in (Asano 2004).

On the other hand, an algorithm (even which is commonly used) should not be used in areas where a high degree of security is needed, if there are facts of the existence of undesirable vulnerabilities in it (and, surely, if the algorithm was broken). For example, some of the widely used hash-functions: MD2, MD4, MD5, HAVAL-128 — are proven to be not acceptable one-way functions (simply stated, are broken) (Muller 2004; Wang et al. 2004), and therefore, in order to provide a greater security level, should be replaced by functions not already broken.

Summarising the information in this section, one should not use a personally created or modified cryptographic algorithm, as well as, where possible and necessary, one should not use algorithms that are proven to be insecure (i. e. broken). The solution is to use trusted non-broken yet cryptographic algorithms (Schneier 1999).

Errors in implementing cryptographic algorithms

Even if a mathematical model of an algorithm (or a protocol) has been proven to be secure, it is not guaranteed that an implementation of the algorithm is also secure.

If in the software development, cryptographic algorithms are written from null, then an errors in the implementation of cryptographic algorithms are programming errors — errors of an improper mapping of operations and logics of algorithms to the source code by software programmers. Programming errors in cryptographic software include the following errors:

- *bugs* — which are common for the entire programming and not specific to cryptography; methods for controlling them are not discussed here separately;
- *usage of cryptographic algorithms in an improper way* — see chapter 3.3.
- *usage of improper algorithms* — for example, if a stream cipher assumes a PRNG to be used, then there should be used only *cryptographically secure* PRNGs, but not simple generators which are built in some programming languages (e. g. the function *std::rand()* in C++).

To avoid most of programming errors in implementation of cryptographic algorithms, and to simplify and shorten the implementation process, there are provided a number of cryptographic libraries with implementations of commonly used (and sometimes also many other, not so popular) cryptographic algorithms.

However, if in software development, some cryptographic algorithms have been already implemented in cryptographic software libraries, then there is a possibility that there exist errors or vulnerabilities in these libraries. A distinctive feature of this type of vulnerabilities is that in many cases (e. g. when the libraries being used are of closed source) these vulnerabilities cannot be discovered by a person who uses the library. In addition to this, vulnerabilities in commonly used software (including software platforms and APIs) are regularly discovered.

Although vulnerabilities in software libraries and platforms exist, due to an amount of efforts devoted to finding the vulnerabilities and correcting the corresponding errors, it remains a better way to implement a cryptographic algorithm rather than by a programmer itself. Moreover, many of these software libraries and platform are in the state of continuous development, and therefore, normally there are released patches or updates, which eliminate the vulnerabilities found.

Usage of cryptographic algorithms in an improper way

An example of improper use of already implemented algorithms is the following. If an algorithm uses a pseudo-random number generator (PRNG), it should not be forgotten to be seeded; the seed shall not be constant, but be as random as possible. Therefore, if in an implementation of a cryptographic algorithm there is used an already implemented routine, its specification and considerations of using it should be studied.

This problem has a considerably effective solution in object-oriented programming languages. Because of the property of encapsulation and existence of constructors and destructors (or finalisers) in these languages, it is much easier to enforce the program to behave more or less desirably. For example, it is possible to make the program set a seed value for PRNG at the first time when a PRNG is called (by encapsulating into a class which implements PRNG a call counter); however, if a language without an encapsulation (and thus non-object-oriented) is used, it is possible to cheat (deliberately or accidentally) this safety mechanism (e. g. by modifying a value of the counter).

Unaccounted specific features of the external environment

One such vulnerability can occur if an operating system which uses a swapping, moves (i. e. swaps out) data from the program's memory to the disk. If in the data swapped out there was a confidential information (such as a private key), and the computer at the moment when this information was on a hard drive was abnormally terminated, the confidential information will be available on the hard drive for an undefined period of time — which is a potential security threat (Ferguson, Schneier 2003). In order to eliminate such a risk, an implementation of a cryptographic method shall take actions to prevent swapping the confidential information out to the disk (e. g. using a special system calls). By using self-implemented cryptographic routines or some immature cryptographic libraries, there is a risk of the program being insecure.

IMPLEMENTATION OF CRYPTOGRAPHY USING SOFTWARE LIBRARIES AND FRAMEWORKS

There exist a plenty of cryptographic libraries. Some of them implement a few cryptographic algorithms, but some of them (like Botan, Crypto++) implement a variety of cryptographic algorithms. Cryptographic libraries differ from each other also by the language or software platform they were written for. For example, the Cryptlib library is written in non-object-oriented language C, and can be used by the programs written in mainly C/C++. There also exist software frameworks which have an implementation of commonly used cryptographic algorithms: Microsoft .NET Framework and Java Platform Standard Edition (Java SE). .NET framework can be used by any CLI language (C#, Visual Basic for .NET, Delphi for .NET, C++/CLI, etc.), and Java SE can be used by the Java programming language and some other programming languages (see below).

Further in this chapter, there given solutions of what cryptographic frameworks (including libraries) can be used for some of the languages; also some commonly used cryptographic libraries are compared with each other.

Possibilities of using cryptographic frameworks in languages with no native support of cryptography

For some programming languages, there exist slight modifications (ports) of these languages to make them support the Microsoft .NET Framework, the Java Platform or another software framework — so-called *managed* versions of the corresponding programming languages. For such managed programming languages, porting enables them to use the entire cryptographic (as long as other) functionality provided by these software frameworks.

For some natively unmanaged programming languages (and, theoretically, for the natively managed languages whose frameworks do not provide a cryptographic functions), there exist cryptographic libraries that are implemented in these languages. An amount and a functionality of such libraries vary from one language to another (surely, depending also on the popularity of the language) — for example, for the C++ language, there exist many cryptographic libraries, however, for the Ada language, very few native (that are written in Ada) cryptographic libraries exist.

Therefore, for some languages, in order to use reliable and secure cryptographic functions, generally the only possible way is, instead of using the native (unmanaged) language, to use a port of the language to a framework which provides cryptographic functions needed. In this way, cryptographic functionality can be implemented in a variety of languages: languages which have their Common Language Infrastructure (CLI) implementations: e. g. C++ (which has a managed version named C++/CLI), Delphi (respectively Delphi.NET), Java (J#), Python (IronPython), Ruby (IronRuby), Lisp (L#, IronLisp), PHP (Phalanger), Prolog (P#) (dotnetpowered.com 2008); and languages which have their Java Virtual Machine (JVM) implementations: e. g. Python (Jython), Ruby (JRuby), JavaScript (Rhino), Scheme (Bigloo, Kawa, SISC), Haskell (Jaskell) (Tolksdorf 2008).

It needs no saying that a cryptographic functionality of the software frameworks can be used by programming languages which are *natively* managed by the corresponding virtual machines, such as Java, C# and VB.NET.

Comparison of major cryptographic frameworks

In this section, some commonly used cryptographic libraries and frameworks which provide cryptographic functionality are compared with each other. This comparison is an instrument to construct some guidelines for selecting a feasible solution for the implementation of cryptographic algorithms in software.

The main static criterion used for the comparison of some major cryptographic frameworks is the functionality of the corresponding framework — i. e. a presence or a lack of support for some common cryptographic algorithms. However, the static criteria of comparison also include operating systems and programming languages supported by the solution. It should be noted that all cryptographic libraries compared have an object-oriented architecture. The result of the comparison is shown in Table 3. For the comparison, there were used the specifications of the frameworks, as well as the results of personal experiments.

Class of algorithm	Algorithm	Cryptographic framework / library:				
		Java SE 6	.NET Framework 3.5	Crypto++ 5.6.0	Botan 1.8.2	Bouncy Castle
Hash-function	MD-5	+	+	+	+	+
	SHA-1	+	+	+	+	+
	SHA-256	+	+	+	+	+
	SHA-384	+	+	+	+	+
	SHA-512	+	+	+	+	+
	RIPEMD160	–	+	+	+	+
	other	–	–	Tiger, Whirlpool et al.	Tiger, Whirlpool et al.	–
Block cipher	AES (Rijndael)	+	+	+	+	+
	RC2	+	+	+	+	+
	Triple DES	+	+	+	+	+
	other	Blowfish	–	RC6, Blowfish, Twofish, Serpent et al.	RC6, Blowfish, Twofish, Serpent et al.	Blowfish
Stream cipher	ARC4	+	–	+	+	+

Class of algorithm	Algorithm	Cryptographic framework / library:				
		Java SE 6	.NET Framework 3.5	Crypto++ 5.6.0	Botan 1.8.2	Bouncy Castle
	other	–	–	Salsa20, Panama u. c.	Salsa20 u. c.	–
Asymmetrical ciphers		RSA	RSA	RSA, ElGamal	RSA, ElGamal	RSA
Natively supported programming languages:		Java, JRuby, Jython, Scala and other JVM languages	C#, VB.NET, Delphi.NET, C++/CLI and other CLI languages	C++	C++	C#, Java
Supported operating systems:		cross-platform	cross-platform (for systems other than Windows, the .NET-compliant Mono platform can be used)	cross-platform		

Table 3.   A comparison of several major cryptographic software frameworks by static criteria

By analysing the results of the comparison, one can conclude that all cryptographic frameworks compared support nearly all widespread cryptographic algorithms (and *all* most widespread algorithms); as well as all cryptographic frameworks are platform-independent and have similar design principles. These conclusions show the fact that when one needs to select a specific cryptographic framework, the choice is mostly influenced by the programming language used, as well as by other non-static criteria of cryptographic frameworks (mostly, by the speed rate of algorithms — see further in this chapter).

In figures 1 and 2, there are shown the results of a comparison of three cryptographic frameworks: Java SE, .NET Framework and Botan, by the speed of execution of their implemented algorithms.

For the measurement of speed, by the authors there were written three similar test programs — a program in Java for Java SE framework, a program in C# for .NET Framework, and a program in C++ for Botan library. To maximally smooth over the differences between results, in every program each cryptographic algorithm was called with data with different size — from 32 B to 32 MB. To measure small amounts of time with a high precision, each cryptographic algorithm with the same input data size was called many times in a loop. Before calling cryptographic algorithms, all input data have been completely loaded into the RAM. After the amount of time needed for a cryptographic algorithm to complete has been measured, a relative speed of execution (in megabytes-of-input-data-per-second) of cryptographic algorithms was calculated; in diagrams, there are shown average values of the corresponding speeds. The test programs were executed on a computer with an Intel Core2Duo 2.20 GHz CPU, 4 GB RAM, and Microsoft Windows XP SP3 operating system.

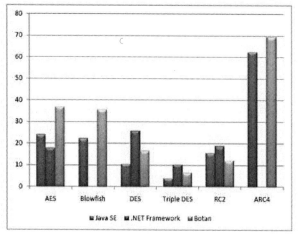

Figure 1. A speed rate of symmetrical ciphers in different cryptographic frameworks (MB/s)

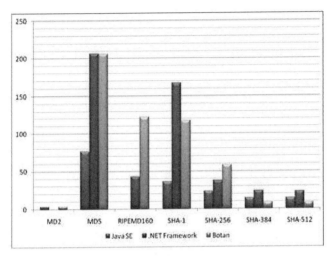

Figure 2. A speed rate of hash functions in different cryptographic frameworks (MB/s)

By comparing an average speed rate of *hash functions* in frameworks Java SE and Microsoft .NET Framework, one can see that hash algorithms implemented in .NET Framework in all cases are faster than in Java SE. Implementations of hash functions SHA-256, SHA-384 and SHA-512 in .NET Framework are about 40% faster than in Java SE; but implementations of hash functions MD5 un SHA-1 in .NET Framework is about 3 times faster than in Java SE.

By analysing the dependence of time needed for hash functions to run, one can conclude that on data of almost any size (starting from 1 KB), a speed rate of hash functions (in MB/s) is approximately constant.

There are some uncharacteristic results for all block symmetric ciphers implemented in .NET Framework, except for an AES algorithm. By analysing theoretical knowledge about block cipher modes of operation, it is clear that all widespread modes of operation are similar in terms of a number of basic computational operations needed to implement them. Therefore, there should not be a significant difference between speed rates of different modes of operation for the same block cipher. This fact is true for all block ciphers implemented in Java SE; however, this is false for block ciphers DES, Triple DES and RC2 in

.NET Framework — here, by unknown cause, a speed rate for mode CFB is many (approximately 7) times smaller than for other modes (furthermore, for other modes, speed rates are approximately the same). This situation for two block ciphers only (AES and Triple DES) in a graphical way is shown in figure 3.

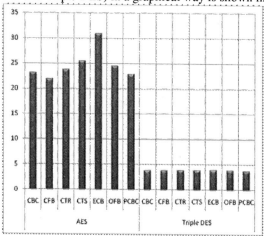

Figure 3.   An average speed rate of some block ciphers depending on their mode of operation, in different cryptographic frameworks (MB/s)

Unlike hash functions, *symmetric ciphers* implemented in Java SE in some cases execute faster than those implemented in .NET Framework. For example, AES implemented in Java SE is about 20% faster than in .NET Framework. Although other ciphers (DES, Triple DES and RC2) in modes CBC and ECB run faster in .NET Framework, the same ciphers in mode CFB run faster in Java SE.

By comparing cryptographic frameworks oriented to *interpreted* (or partially interpreted) languages (Java SE, .NET Framework) and to *compiled* languages (Botan), one can see that the speed rate for all of the compared frameworks in average does not differ significantly. For example, block ciphers AES and Blowfish are faster in programs implemented using Botan, however, this fact is not true for other widespread ciphers. The difference between the speed rates for hash functions in Botan and .NET Framework largely depend on the hash function itself.

It is important to notice that during practical experiments with the test programs, there was determined that all corresponding cryptographic frameworks (Java SE 6, .NET Framework 3.5 and Botan 1.8.2) do not have a native support of multi-core processors.

POSSIBILITIES OF MAXIMISING A SPEED OF EXECUTION OF CRYPTOGRAPHIC ALGORITHMS

In software where cryptographic algorithms are widely used, a speed of execution of cryptographic algorithms is of a big importance. A bottleneck for the speed of execution of cryptographic algorithms usually is a processor on which these algorithms are executed. Therefore, in order to efficiently maximise the speed of execution of these algorithms, a processing unit should be used to the extent possible.

It is important to note that many modern computers have video cards that can also be used for arbitrary (even not related with graphics) calculations, including cryptographic algorithms. This technique of using graphic processing units (GPUs) for general-purpose calculations is called *general-purpose computing on graphics processing units (GPGPU)*. GPU developers provide free GPU programming libraries (or SDKs), e. g. OpenCL (Open Computing Language), CUDA by Nvidia, Stream SDK by AMD.

Most modern processing systems (CPUs and GPUs) are multi-core processors. Modern GPUs, in contrast with CPUs, are composed of a large number of cores (of the order of several tens). (Moreover, a computational power of GPUs in average is not less than a computational power of CPUs.) This means that multi-core CPUs, as well as GPUs provide a big possibility for speeding up an execution of cryptographic algorithms. In order to take advantage of using multi-core processors, cryptographic algorithms should be adapted for parallel execution. However, as there was discovered by the authors (see chapter 4.2), most widespread frameworks which provide a cryptographic functionality do not support advantages of multi-core processors (neither they support advantages of multi-core CPUs, nor they have a support of GPUs). This means that (at least at the moment of writing this paper) in order to get a greater performance of cryptographic algorithms, one should implement all needed cryptographic algorithms *manually*, or should use some raw third-party implementations of these algorithms. At least for some time, this way of implementing cryptographic algorithms cannot be guaranteed to be secure to a certain degree.

Not all cryptographic algorithms can be easily adapted to be executed efficiently on multi-core processors. However, in the master's project, there was emphasized that *block ciphers* (which are the ciphers used mostly, and, possibly, the cryptographic primitives used mostly) in the CTR mode of operation are both embarrassingly parallel (i. e. they can easily be separated in a number of parallel tasks) and enough secure. This means that for at least one class of cryptographic algorithms, there exists a possibility to *significantly* speed up their execution on modern computers; a gain of an execution speed will mostly depend on a number of cores in a processing unit.

CONCLUSIONS

The main conclusions of the research can be formulated as follows:

- Conclusions about a secure implementation of cryptographic algorithms:
    - o The reason for most errors in an implementation of cryptographic algorithms is an inadequate knowledge of base principles and methods of cryptography, a use of unsafe (broken) cryptographic algorithms, as well as a human factor.
    - o In order to implement secure software with cryptographic functionality, one shall consider a program execution mechanism and a specificity of an operating system.
- Conclusions about a usage of cryptographic frameworks in software development:
    - o All widespread cryptographic libraries support most widely used cryptographic algorithms, and therefore are similar in terms of their functionality.
    - o There exist wide possibilities to use cryptographic frameworks also from non-native programming languages.
    - o In general case, it is not true that cryptographic algorithms implemented in software libraries written in compiled languages (e. g. C++) are faster than algorithms implemented in software platforms Java SE and Microsoft .NET Framework.
- Conclusions about a speed of execution of cryptographic algorithms:

o None of cryptographic frameworks compared can be considered as the fastest — the rank of each framework can be different depending on a specific cryptographic algorithm.
o Multi-core central processing units and also graphics processing units can be used to speed up the execution of cryptographic algorithms several times.
o Cryptographic frameworks analysed do not have a native support of multi-core processors.
o If there is needed a faster implementation of cryptographic algorithms than cryptographic frameworks compared provide, one shall implement these algorithms manually, using the advantages of processing system. However, in this situation, the resulting security level can be very low.

The paper is addressed to specialists in computer science who are interested in a secure and fast software implementation of cryptographic algorithms.

REFERENCES

Asano, T. (2004), "Secure and Insecure Modifications of the Subset Difference Broadcast Encryption Scheme" in *Lecture Notes in Computer Science*, 3108, p. 12–23.

Black, J., Cochran, M., and Highland, T. (2006), "A Study of the MD5 Attacks: Insights and Improvements", <http://www.cs.colorado.edu/~jrblack/papers/md5e-full.pdf>.

dotnetpowered.com (2008), "dotnetpowered Language List", <http://www.dotnetpowered.com/languages.aspx>.

Ferguson, N., Schneier, B. (2003), "Practical Cryptography", John Wiley & Sons.

Muller F. (2004), "The MD2 Hash Function Is Not One-Way" in *Lecture Notes in Computer Science*, 3329, p. 214–229.

Nazaruks, V. (2009), "Kriptogrāfisko algoritmu realizēšanas analīze programmatūras izstrādē", in *Lietišķās datorsistēmas*, p. 56–61, Latvia, Riga.

Schneier, B. (1996), "Applied Cryptography", 2nd Edition, John Wiley & Sons.

Schneier, B. (1999), "Cryptography: The Importance of Not Being Different", <http://www.schneier.com/essay-189.html>.

Stevens, M., Lenstra, A., and de Weger, B. (2007), "Vulnerability of software integrity and code signing applications to chosen-prefix collisions for MD5" <http://www.win.tue.nl/hashclash/SoftIntCodeSign/>.

Tolksdorf, R. (2008), "Robert Tolksdorf's Programming Languages for the Java Virtual Machine", <http://www.is-research.de/info/vmlanguages/>.

Wang, X., Feng, D., Lai, X., and Yu H. (2004), "Collisions for Hash Functions MD4, MD5, HAVAL-128 and RIPEMD", <http://www.insidepro.com/doc/199.pdf>.

EVALUATION OF IMMERSIVE LEARNING PROJECTS

Fred Kitchens

Miller College of Business, Ball State University, Muncie, Indiana, USA,
fkitchens@bsu.edu

ABSTRACT

Systems Analysis and Design is taught in a two-semester sequence by the author in the Information Systems curriculum. Using an Immersive- or Service-Learning approach, the students work in a consulting capacity with local businesses to solve an Information Systems related problem. A common question from colleagues and students alike, concerns the grading methods used in evaluation of the student projects. This paper discusses the background of the type of learning which occurs in these projects, and discusses six evaluation methods used by the author.

Keywords: *Immersive Learning, Service Learning, Evaluation, Grading, Peer Evaluation, kinaesthetic.*

INTRODUCTION

Service learning, service learning, experiential learning, and immersive learning; by whatever definition is used all have a common feature. They involve students working on a project, generally for an outside client, in a hands-on fashion. At the author's university, Immersive Learning is closely related to service learning. By definition, Immersive Learning conforms to seven principles (Gora, 2006):

1. A group of students, preferably interdisciplinary, working collaboratively
2. Work under the guidance of a faculty mentor
3. Students drive the learning process, determining the direction of the project
4. Students work with community partners
5. The experience produces a tangible outcome or product such as a business venture, DVD, or creative work that is a benefit to the community and to the students

6. Provides students with an industry connection

7. Students receive academic credit

In the Information Systems major at the author's university, there is a 2-semester sequence of courses in Systems Analysis and Design. These constitute a capstone project for the students in the major. Because the course Information Systems major is located in the College of Business, students are given a basic technical education is areas such as networking, database, security, ecommerce, etc... But, they are not given the depth of technical skills that they might get in other majors such as Computer Science or Technology. For this reason, the capstone is taught from an IT consulting standpoint with a business focus, rather than from a detailed technical perspective. Projects completed by previous students include things like; a designing a paperless clinic for the local hospital, a Business Continuity and Security plan for the local city government; proposing an Enterprise Resource Planning system for a local manufacturer, designing an inventory control system for a local retail store.

By their very nature, these projects have no pre-existing solution. The students are taught the principles of the Systems Development Lifecycle (Gido & Clements 2003; VanHorn, Schwarzkopf & Price, 2006; Dennis & Wixom, 2003). They are lead through a process of investigating the existing as-in system, developing a problem statement, and assessing the business processes in place. Then, they design the most appropriate solution for the client.

Some professors have expressed concern over the lack of pre-defined solution; to the point that some will avoid assigning such projects in class. The concern is over the grading methods used to evaluate a solution for which there is no 'perfect' answer. This paper attempts to provide some solutions to the problems associated with grading hands-on projects such as Immersive Learning.

BACKGROUND, DEVELOPMENT, AND LITERATURE REVIEW

Fleming developed four categories by which people learn: visual, auditory, reading/writing, and kinaesthetic (Fleming, 1992). The traditional classroom setting where students sit, listen, and take notes during a lecture or demonstration is conducive to the auditory, reading/writing, and to some extent the visual styles of learning. But the kinaesthetic style of learning is largely ignored except for situations such as lab experiments and science projects involving field-work. This is where service learning is able to help bridge the gap. Service learning, by nature, involves kinaesthetic, hands-on, developmental project-based work.

Because this style of teaching is rather less-traditional, the question often is raised as to how to evaluate and assign a grade to projects in which lecturing is de-emphasized (but not eliminated) and students' participation and interaction with the real-world is encouraged. When there is no pre-determined answer, how do you know if the students got it right or not? The answer is rather simple. The implementation becomes a little bit harder.

The instructor in these situations needs to watch and evaluate the procedures that are followed in the course of the students' coming up with an answer. If the procedures are followed properly, then the solution, by default, should be sound. For the instructor, this involves much more than matching multiple choice answers with an answer key, or even reading essays to find the proper answer to an application-type question. Evaluating the process requires watching and witnessing the procedures as they are completed; reviewing the corresponding documentation, and asking the right (often clever) questions of the right people.

METHODS

The author has developed a multi-tier approach to evaluating student immersive learning projects in order to assign a grade. The tiers include:

0   The client's input
- The student teams documentation of the procedures
- The instructor's evaluation of each student's participation
- Quantitative student peer evaluations
- Exams with traditional questions
- Exams with non-traditional questions

Combined, these five items provide a well-rounded evaluation of each student. The objective is to measure both; participation and more importantly the education gained from participation.

The client's input

There are no points associated with this portion of the evaluation; but the client's input is the largest determinant in the student's grade. Following the Systems Development Lifecycle; after the Analysis phase of the project the students present their findings to the client. They discuss their plan for completing the project, the direction in which they plan to look for a solution (off-the-shelf solution, third-party hosting, outsourced development, or in-house development), and any resources they will require from the client (such as their time and access to information). The two parties sign a letter of agreement, clearly identifying the students' responsibilities and defining the final deliverable.

At the conclusion of the project, students present their final deliverable in a formal business presentation to the client. Following the presentation and the question and answer session, the instructor turns to the client and asks, "Are you satisfied that they have delivered a satisfactory product, based on your agreement?" If the client says, "Yes," then the instructor will grade the project. If they say, "No," then the project will not be graded, and a 'zero' will be assigned for that portion of the course grade. The author chooses to weight this portion of the students' grade at forty percent.

This method virtually creates a 'Pass/Fail' environment. However, it also allows the professor to assign a grade, without allowing the client any leeway in the grading scale. The method is intended to simulate a business environment where the client will either pay for the product, or reject the product.

The instructor's evaluation of each student's participation

At the end of the semester, the author asks each student to write a memo, stating the grade they feel they deserve, and justifying that grade by explaining their efforts throughout the semester. The author also states that he will group the memos according to team membership before reading them, so that he can watch for discrepancies (such as three people claiming to have done the same work). The students who have truly done the work have no problem completing the assignment. There are always a few who need to pad the memo with frivolous tasks which were not associated directly with the project, and obviously not assigned to them by the team. Having completed such tasks as picking-up take-out food for the team, driving team members home, and even resolving group conflict; were likely not assigned as project-related tasks by the team.

More than anything else, this assignment helps individual team members to realize that even though the teams' project might have been successful, their individual grade may be lower than they expected. Often, they begin to anticipate that their individual grade will be low, before they actually receive the course grade.

The student teams documentation of the procedures

Throughout the 2-semester project, the students' reports are submitted for grading at least 5 times, using a phase-gate approach. This provides the instructor an opportunity to grade and provide feedback on each phase. The report then grows cumulatively over time, improving with each round of feedback.

Observing the project at various stages, as it grows and develops into a professional document, allows the instructor to assess the students' ability to apply the SDLC procedures in a proper fashion. The 'solution' is not what is being graded. Indeed, there is no 'perfect' solution to the type of real-world problems that the student teams are solving. However, the students will arrive at a 'good' solution if the SDLC steps are followed properly. The ability to follow the SDLC steps properly is what is being graded.

Quantitative student peer evaluations

Peer evaluations are the subject of debate and controversy. Students frequently attempt to manipulate the peer rating system with team-agreements to 'rate everyone a 10 out of 10' or, for factions within a team to rate other team members poorly. Aside from manipulation schemes, students often fall victim to cognitive biases such as the Horn effect (Thorndike, 1920), Egocentric bias (Ross & Sicoly, 1979), Ingroup bias (Tajfel, 1970), Primacy effect (Asch, 1946), Recency effect (Murdock, 1962), and other common problems associated with peer evaluations.

To overcome the common problems associated with peer evaluations, the author created a quantitative scoring system based on nine questions relating to team member performance and professionalism. (Additional comments are encouraged, but are not used in the numeric evaluation. Comments are used to provide additional feedback to students if they question the peer evaluation score they are assigned.) The numeric scores assigned by each teammate are entered in a spreadsheet which first standardizes the scores, then indexes them. The highest-ranked student on the team is thereby assigned 100%, an all other teammates are rated down from 100. This system removes nearly all possibility of student manipulating the system, overcomes much of the bias, and provides a consistent set of scores between multiple teams in a single course.

The author's experience reveals two things about this system peer evaluations: First, the students consistently rank their peers in nearly the same order that the author expects based on his (limited) observation of the work they perform together. Second, the system reveals the brutal honesty with which students consistently rate each other.

The mathematics used in this system (standardizing and indexing) produces sores which fit neatly in a standard 90-80-70-60% grading scale. As a rule of thumb, a team's scores usually 30-40% in the "A" range, 40-50% in the "B" range, and 10-20% in the "C" range, and an occasional student in the "D" or "F" range.

Exams with traditional questions

Traditional exams are used during the semester to test individual student's knowledge of the theory and application of various systems analysis and design principles. Because so much of the course is based on group-work, individual exams provide a means of distributing the grades within each team, and flushing out the students who really know, or really do not know the material.

Exams with non-traditional questions

The author uses a final exam with 'unexpected' questions as a final method of determining which students actually performed the work and understood the project. Students are told, "The exam will be based on each team's specific project. If you actively engaged in the project during the semester, the exam will be easy."

Student answers to the questions are graded based on the specific content of the team's report, or based on comparing answers between teammates. Questions, for example, might include:

- Write a 1 (or 2) paragraph Executive Summary of your team's report.
- Describe the first meeting with the client. What was discussed? What decisions were made? Where was the meeting held? What did the client look like?
- What Information Gathering techniques were used? Which team members were responsible for each technique? What was learned using each technique?
- List three risks associated with your team's project, and how they are mitigated.
- List the tasks that were assigned to each team member, and describe the result was.

CONCLUSIONS

There are pros and cons to adopting a teaching method which engages immersive projects, or service learning. The cons include wore work for the instructor, coordination with a business or outside client, difficulty pleasing the client, and difficulty grading students on work for which there is no 'perfect' answer.

On the other hand, the author feels that the pros include a better educational experience for the students (better than using academic case studies for example), support for the local community, higher job-placement rate for the students, and intrinsic rewards for the instructor. Overall, the author feels that the pros outweigh the cons.

With non-traditional teaching methods, it is a logical conclusion that one might have to use non-traditional grading procedures. Grading immersive projects is not a matter of checking to see if the answer is correct. Rather, it is a system of monitoring the procedures that are followed to arrive at a good and appropriate conclusion. The author has shared six instruments used in his evaluation process, most of which are somewhat non-traditional in their application or approach.

REFERENCES

Asch, S. E. (1946) Forming impressions of personality, Journal of Abnormal and Social Psychology, 41, 258-290

Dennis, A. & Wixon, B.H. (2003), "Systems Analysis and Design; an Applied Approach", 2nd Edition, John Wiley & Sons, Inc., USA.

Fleming, N.D. and Mills, C. (1992), Not Another Inventory, Rather a Catalyst for Reflection, To Improve the Academy, Vol. 11, 1992., page 137.

Gido, J. & Clements, J.P. (2003), "Successful Project management," 2nd Edition, Thomson Learning, USA.

Gora, J.A., "President Gora's fall 2006 faculty/staff convocation remarks" Emens Auditorium, 8/18/2006, www.bsu.edu.

Murdock, B.B., Jr. (1962) The Serial Position Effect of Free Recall, Journal of Experimental Psychology, 64, 482-488.

Ross, M. & Sicoly, F. (1979). Egocentric biases in availability and attribution. Journal of Personality and Social Psychology 37, 322-336.

Tajfel, H. (1970). Experiments in intergroup discrimination. Scientific American, 223, 96-102.

Thorndike, E. L. (1920). A constant error on psychological rating. Journal of Applied Psychology, IV, 25-29

VanHorn, R.L., Schwarzkopf, A.B., & Price, R.L. (2006), "Information Systems Solutions; A Project Approach", McGraw-Hill Irwin, New York, NY.

EFFICIENCY EVALUATION SYSTEM OF STEGANALYSIS METHODS

Vladimir Ambrosov, Andrey Yershov

Faculty of Computer Science and Information Technology, Riga Technical University, Riga, Latvia

{vladimirs.ambrosovs | aayershov}@rtu.lv

ABSTRACT

This article offers solution for the problem of efficiency evaluation of steganalysis methods. It describes nature of steganalysis, which is connected with steganography, as well as several types of steganalysis. System for evaluating efficiency of steganalysis methods was elaborated on the base of this description. 10 properties are defined during the development stage; they are called the criteria of the evaluation system. Every criterion is characterised with value which can be calculated by usage of given formulas. Achieved results are represented as a diagram. After graphical analysis it is possible to compute values of efficiency by calculating the area of the diagram. In the end the, application of the elaborated system is shown in test example.

Keywords: Steganography, steganalysis, security, privacy.

INTRODUCTION

Nowadays, when information technologies develop fast, the significance of the information is important and more attention is given to its protection. From olden times people tried to protect information. Origins of the cryptographic science with its aim to hide information were set by human desire to solve problem of information security. Later the steganography emerged, which is a science with an aim to hide the fact of the existence of the message. Both sciences developed parallel and influenced each other. Nowadays they are still closely connected.

This article is based on scientific research with a scope of hidden information recognition methods and evaluation according to defined system of criteria.

The area of this research is related to steganography. The word "steganography" is formed by two Greek words: stegos – hidden from perception – and graphein – to write. Nowadays steganography is widely used in IT sphere, and multiple algorithms and approaches to digital data hiding exist (for example, photo, video and audio LSB, model driven embedding techniques, F5 hiding algorithm etc.) [1]. The research of steganography is being made in Riga Technical University as well. The facts for that can be found in the article describing the comparative analysis of two steganographic methods – LSB and Kutter [2].

People have always tried to expose something that is hidden. Cryptography has its antithesis – cryptanalysis, similarly steganography has its opposition – steganalysis [3]. Basically, steganalysis is more complicated than steganography, because hiding the existence of information is easier than extracting it. Multiple types of attacks on hidden data exist. Moreover, efficiency of each type is described both by advantages and disadvantages.

Steganalysis is relatively new science, that is why there are no systems which are able to determine whether the method is effective or not [4]. Regardless of this fact, the areas of steganalysis application can be easily found: international espionage, information system protection, antiterrorism activities, digital forensics etc.

Despite there are various steganalysis methods and tools, the literature barely describes how their efficiency and security could be evaluated. This is the problem of steganalysis, because every method's effectiveness varies depending on the situation [4]. As the solution to this problem, the author of the article offers the evaluation system elaborated during the research, which can help to perform comparative analysis of steganalysis methods, i.e., evaluate the methods and choose the most suitable identifying covert information according to given requirements.

STEGANALYSIS

The digital data hiding process makes changes to the properties of the cover work [5]. The main idea of steganalysis is the detection of these changes. Requirements for the methods significantly change depending on situation, because the data embedding or hiding algorithm, type of cover work, volume of hidden data and other factors should be taken into account when choosing the right approach to perform an attack on the steganographic system.

Hidden information recognition

The main idea of the steganalysis hides in the understanding the steganography. Steganalysis is inverse to steganographic systems, that is why, to understand steganalysis methods, it is important to comprehend the steganographic scheme [1].

The functioning of the steganographic system can be shown in basic situation which is called "the prisoner's problem" [6]. There are two prisoners in jail – Alice and Bob. They are being watched by the guard (Figure 1). The prisoners' main goal is to communicate in such a way, that guard wouldn't be able to find out about their escape plan [6].

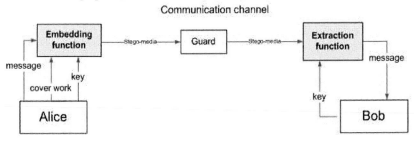

Figure 1. Message steganographic transmitting to Bob [1]

In this situation the guard is equivalent to a steganalysis specialist. He is inseparable piece of the communication channel so it influences the channel properties [1].

The primary goal of the steganalysis is to discover the existence of hidden data. It is considered to be an attack on steganographic system [7]. However, analyst can also have an aim to extract the message or destroy it. Information, which is known to him, influences the process of steganalysis. There are possible 4 information availability scenarios. The steganalysis specialist can have access either only to the stego-media, or both the stego-media with the cover work original, or the stego-media with the embedding algorithm, or even to all three components [7].

The last scenario is the most suitable for the steganalysis, because it provides all the necessary information for realising a successful attack. In other scenarios it is also possible to analyze the stego-media object, but the probability of successful attack decreases.

Steganalysis methods

Two types of steganalysis exist: blind steganalysis and targeted steganalysis. Blind steganalysis is an approach when the method of steganography, which was used for stego-media object creation, is not known [3]. In that case the guard has general understanding about the existing algorithms and based on this knowledge he tries to perform an attack. Unlike the blind steganalysis, in the targeted steganalysis the guard knows the embedding function that is why the method is targeted to the particular steganographic algorithm.

There is at least one steganalysis method for every steganographic algorithm [4]. The most primitive techniques of steganalysis are visual and acoustic methods. Steganographic methods, that hide data in BMP, JPEG, MP3, AVI and other multimedia formats, become popular and spread all over the world nowadays [8].

Multimedia data containers have a property that can be used for recognizing hidden message with visual and acoustic methods. Graphical files can have obvious quality distortion but audio files can contain noises. Those signs create suspicions about the existence of hidden data in the data container. These methods belong to blind steganalysis because hiding algorithm is not known. Blind steganalysis includes also JPEG picture calibration method and spatial area method. JPEG calibration method is based on statistic analysis of picture properties, but second method – on spatial area statistics of the picture [1].

Histogram attack method belongs to the targeted steganalysis type. Given method is used for "*Least Significant Bit*" (LSB) steganographic embedding. Basically LSB method hides message in not significant bit sequences of cover work. More information about LSB can be found in the information source [2]. Histogram attack method uses asymmetry which is formed in even and odd pixel embedding process. When pixel histogram is analysed with statistic methods, one can say if there is embedded message in the picture [3].

EVALUATION SYSTEM

The main problem of steganalysis is impossibility to estimate effectiveness of methods in particular situation. The system elaborated in presented research is intended for solving this problem.

Steganalysis software usually includes several steganalysis methods, which makes those tools more effective. Elaborated system is useful both for separate steganalysis methods and for software solutions. The main difference is that, comparing steganalysis software, evaluated tools can use the same steganalysis method. This gives an opportunity to compare one method's different implementations, which are presented as software solutions.

The development of the evaluation system is stepwise. It is necessary to define the list of criteria at first, which will be used for steganalysis methods evaluation. To unite the values of the criteria, it is important to define the method of graphical representation and the formula for efficiency evaluation. The last step means the description of marking out the properties for etalon method out of the achieved results.

Criteria

To develop the evaluation system, which could help to estimate efficiency of steganalysis methods, the author of this article defines, in his opinion, the most important properties of steganalysis methods and offers using them as the system criteria. Each criterion is given a formula, to calculate its numeric value.

Before defining the criteria, the author states, that the defined formulas for calculating numeric values are based on mathematical dependencies, proportions and percentages but does not reflect mathematical laws. The main purpose of these values is to give possibility to compare multiple methods of steganalysis. That is why the formulas cannot be used for calculations outside the boundaries of the evaluation system.

Algorithm dependency

There are steganalysis methods, which are targeted to detecting only one steganographic algorithm as well as those, which are able to detect multiple embedding algorithms. This criterion describes the number of algorithms, which can expose the given method of steganalysis. The numeric value of the targeted steganalysis methods is equal to the number of algorithms it was developed to detect. It is known, because the targeted steganalysis is based on the known embedding algorithms. When it comes to blind steganalysis methods, their numeric value is based on the number of steganographic algorithms they can possibly detect. This statement involves the fact, that each steganographic algorithm changes a property of the cover work. Blind steganalysis methods are designed to detect these property changes, so every steganographic algorithm, which changes particular property, can be detected by the blind steganalysis method, and the numeric value of the described criterion is equal to the number of embedding algorithms, which change the particular property of the cover work. The author proposes labelling the algorithm dependency criterion with a variable R.

If the steganalysis tools are compared using the elaborated system, the numeric value is equal to the number of steganographic algorithms the given program supports. Usually, this number is given in the software interface or in its documentation.

Classification dependency

There are different cover work classes in digital steganography. The author of the article uses the term "class" to describe the type of the data container, which is used as a cover work. Photo, audio, video, text and executable files can be used as a cover work, as well as other types of containers.

The classification dependency clarifies what classes of cover work can be processed using the given steganalysis method. For example, with the help of one method it is possible to detect stego-media only in pictures, but with the help of the other method – both pictures and audio files. The numeric value is equal to number of suitable classes. The author of this article labels the criterion with a variable K.

Format dependency

Every cover work class includes different formats, which have their own properties. This means, that the steganographic method, which supports particular class of the cover work, can be suitable for one format of this class, and can be useless for other formats of a given class. For example, it was discovered in the research during the test of the steganographic tool *S-tools*, that this software is targeted to embedding data into GIF *(Graphics Interchange Format)* and WAV *(Waveform Audio Format)* formats, which belong to different classes. However the software didn't support the embedding into JPEG, MP3 *(MPEG-1 Audio Layer)* and other known graphic and audio formats.

Similarly to steganographic algorithms, steganalysis methods can be suitable only for particular data formats, others for multiple formats. The numeric value is equal to the number of supported formats. The author labels the criterion with a variable G.

Accuracy

As already mentioned, steganalysis methods can be used for achieving different aims. It can be elaborated for hidden information recognition, extraction or destroying. When the hidden data is detected, sometimes, it is necessary to extract the contents of it. Those methods' efficiency depends on the accuracy.

The accuracy criterion defines the precision of the extracted data in comparison with the original data in case when the method is targeted to hidden data extraction or the precision of the detection of the data length, when the method is targeted to covert information recognition. The author labels this property with a variable p.

The formula (1) is defined for calculating the numeric value. It is based on the dependence of the number of extracted bits to number of bits in the original message, when the goal is to extract the covert data. In case, when the goal is to calculate the volume of hidden data, the formula is based on the dependence of the calculated volume to message's original size. The size of the cover work and the volume of data it is able to store, so calculating the single dependence would give a result for only one case. When the cover work changes, the accuracy value may also change. That is why the author offers calculating accuracy value of different volume data containers, and in the end to get the average of those values. The more cover works are tested, the more precise the p value will be.

$$p = \frac{\sum\limits_{i=1}^{N} \frac{s_{i2}}{s_{i1}}}{N}$$

where s_{i1} – number of bits of the recovered message or calculated hidden data volume in bits,

s_{i2} – number of bits in original message,

N – number of chosen covers.

The author of the article offers assuming that the accuracy is equal to 0 if the message volume is not calculated using the given method or tool or the message contents cannot be extracted.

Error probability

Some tests of the steganalysis tools were made during the research. According to those experiments, it is important to state, that steganalysis tools may often give the wrong result. There were tested 3 tools. Out of the 9 results, which were calculated, only 4 were right. That is why error probability is important, especially, when the time is limited, because choosing the wrong tool may result in great time loss and wrong predictions. The method or tool with the smallest error probability should be considered more effective.

Error probability shows the correctness of the steganalysis method or tool results.The author has obtained the formula (2) for calculating the error probability, and labelled the criterion with a variable e.

$$e = \frac{h}{n}$$

where h – number of wrong results

n – number of all results.

To calculate the error probability value, multiple tests with different cover works from the same class and type should be performed. The tests include firstly hiding some data in those cover works, and then trying to detect or extract it using tools or methods which are being tested. Moreover, the number of correct and wrong results should be recorded. It is assumed, that the "correct" result is the positive answer of the steganalysis method or tool when cover work includes embedded covert data or negative when the cover work is empty. The author proposes to call the "wrong" result, if the tested method or tool returns a positive answer, but the cover work does not contain the embedded message, or returns a negative answer, when the hidden data exists in the data container. Similarly as for previously described criterion, the precision of the value depends on the number of tests made. If more cover works are taken for tests, than the error probability can be estimated more precisely.

Statistical detection level

Steganalysis methods are based on the statistical analysis. The main idea is to search the stego-media for the statistical anomalies, and in case those are found, the steganalysis attack is considered to be successful [1]. The statistical anomalies are the result of the changes, which were made to the properties of the cover work during the embedding process. So with the help of statistical analysis it is possible to detect those property changes. We can conclude that the efficiency of steganalysis methods depends on the way the insignificant anomalies can be found. The author offers using this quality and naming it the statistical detection level at which it is possible to find hidden message using the statistical analysis.

In small stego-media object it is harder to find the hidden data with the help of statistical analysis [1]. It can be explained with the fact that the small cover works consist of less number of bits, which means that there is less information for statistical analysis available. That is why author offers using this fact for calculating value of this criterion. Original research is assumed to label the statistical detection level with a variable l and to calculate the numeric values using the following formula (3):

$$\begin{cases} l = \frac{e_2}{e_1}, jf e_1 \neq 0 \wedge e_1 > e_2 \\ l = 1, jf e_1 \leq e_2 \vee e_1 = 0 \end{cases}$$

where e_1 – error probability for the smallest stego-media object.

e_2 – error probability for the largest stego-media object.

To calculate numeric value of this criterion by using formula (3), it is necessary to obtain values e_2 and e_1 by using formula (2). Value e_2 characterizes error probability for stego-media with maximal volume. It is not possible to determine the maximal volume of stego-media as it can be infinite. That is why, the maximal available volume is assumed to be the maximal volume of given stego-medias in particular situation. To its turn, the minimal stego-media volume is the minimal available in current situation. It is allowed to take these values, because the evaluation system is suitable for particular situations. In every particular situation, the minimal and maximal values may be different.

The formula uses the dependence of the error probability of maximal volume stego-media to the error probability of minimal volume stego-media. Taking into consideration the quality of statistical detection in smaller stego-media, it is possible to conclude, that by using formula (2) for calculating e_1 and e_2, the first value should be larger, than the second, as the error probability in smaller cover work, ought to be larger in usual situation. In this case, the criterion value is smaller than 1 but larger than 0. The maximal value for the criterion is 1. It is reached, when error probability in minimal volume stego-media is equal to 0, or e_1 is smaller than e_2. It means that the situation described in the source [1] does not fulfil and the steganalysis method efficiency does not depend on decreasing the volume of stego-media.

Productivity

Steganalysis is time consuming process [4]. That is why, as it was already mentioned, it is important for steganalysis specialist to choose the time-saving method. So the importance of this factor increases or decreases depending on the situation. It isn't correct to compare the method processing time, because this measure depends on processed stego-media volume – when the volume changes, also time of analysis changes because number of processed bits changes.

The author defines the productivity as a criterion to use for estimating how fast the steganalysis method or tool can give necessary results. Criterion describes finished work in time period depending on cover work volume. The author declares that this criterion is important because processing time depends on the algorithm used by the particular method in case of method evaluation, or which steganalysis algorithms are used by particular tool, if tools are being evaluated. In original research it is used to label productivity with variable W. The author suggests calculating the numeric value using the formula (4):

$$W = \frac{b}{t*f}$$

where b – stego-media size in bits,

t – processing time of method or tool,

f – CPU (Central Processing Unit) speed (frequency).

The formula is based on direct dependence between time and speed. Number of bits is divided with this equation because this criterion reflects how much time is needed, depending on frequency, to process one stego-media bit. If the method or tool has stable productivity then, when frequency increases, the processing time will decrease. When the number of bits increases, the processing time for method's analysis also will increase, however it won't influence the CPU frequency. Wherewith, the productivity of each method or tool is a constant value. That is theoretical statement because in the real environment the processing time can be influenced not only by the CPU speed but also by other factors, like memory speed, speed between system components etc. So the author suggests making tests and calculations with all methods using the same CPU, because the main aim of criteria is to obtain values for comparison. In this case all the calculations will be influenced by the same factors which are not used in the formula.

It is possible to calculate method processing time in any available way. In the original research a stego-media object of large volume was taken for estimating the processing time as the processing of a very large stego-media makes the obvious delay, which can be calculated by just using simple chronometer.

Resource usage

In chapter 3.1.7 it was mentioned that the steganalysis specialist should choose the method with the highest productivity. Though, it is important to know, how much resources the method will consume during the process of steganalysis. The author proposes this statement because the amount of used resources influences the costs of applying steganalysis. To describe the value which reflects the amount of used resources, the author defines a criterion "resource usage". It is proposed to label this criterion with a variable C and calculate it using the defined formula (5):

$$C = \frac{P+M}{2}$$

where P – the usage of CPU (in percents),

M – maximum memory allocation that is used in analysis process (in percents).

Formula defined by the author offers calculating mean average percentage of CPU and memory consumption. P and M are the maximal values found during the steganalysis process. Value of the given criterion is not constant and depends on the computer used in every particular situation. As the aim of evaluation system is to find out efficiency in particular case then usage of this criterion is allowed. To get precise results it is suggested to use the same computer for calculating values of resource consumption for every evaluated method or tool. Based on that, other resource values of the computers are not taken into account in this formula.

The author defines this criterion to increase the accuracy of the evaluation system. That gives a possibility to adjust efficiency in such cases, when the evaluation results for methods are similar and the efficiency differences are not significant. The resource usage criterion together with the productivity value gives a valuable estimation. For example, if two methods have similar productivity but the resource usage is different, the conclusion of which one of them is more effective can be stated.

It is possible to calculate the usage of CPU and maximal allocated memory by using any of the available methods. In the research the built-in software of *Windows* operating system *Task Manager* is used, for these calculations. It reflects both necessary values. In future it is planned to develop software that would give calculated values in more handy form than it is possible to get with the help of *Task Manager*.

Necessary information

Chapter 2.1 describes the important aspects of steganalysis as well as the fact that there are four information availability scenarios. Based on this fact, the author defines the criterion "necessary information", which describes how many information sources are needed for steganalysis method or tool to perform successfully. This is important criterion because there are steganalysis methods which base their performance algorithm on comparison of the original cover work and the stego-media. The histogram attack belongs to this type, as it compares the original and modified picture histograms. To use other methods, for example the one described in the source [9], it is necessary to obtain the stego-media object and to know the algorithm used for embedding the hidden data (F5).

In the original research the label of this criterion is variable B. Numeral value of this criterion satisfy one of possible scenarios (what is really necessary):

1. Only the stego-media object.
2. The Stego-media object and the original of the cover work.
3. The Stego-media object and the information about the embedding algorithm.
4. The Stego-media object, the original of the cover work and the information about embedding algorithm.

If the information needed for steganalysis method fits the first statement, then the value is 3. First case is a general result of steganalysis. If it is possible to recognize the hidden message with this method without using additional information, then it can be considered as successful attack. That is why this case is evaluated with the maximal number of points in 3 point scale. When the necessary information is as in second and third case, the value is 2. But if the last, fourth, point is effective then the value of the criterion is 1. This criterion can't take other values.

Usefulness

There are defined criteria which show the accuracy and error probability of the steganalysis methods and tools, however there isn't defined the one, which shows how useful the steganalysis method or software is. If, for example, the particular productivity is calculated, but at the same time for the method with large error probability, that means that in case of the method returning wrong results the process of steganalysis was senseless. That is why the author defines this criterion to reflect how useful the method or software is, according to various factors. The author suggests labelling this criterion with a variable J and calculating it using the formula (6):

$$\begin{cases} J = W * (1 - e), jfe \neq 0 \\ \quad J = W, jfe = 0 \end{cases} \quad (6)$$

where W – productivity,

$\quad e$ – error probability of the tool or method.

The two cases are available for calculating the formula. If the error probability is not equal to 0, then the usefulness can be calculated using the productivity equation multiplied by difference between 1 and error probability, because the usefulness is described with the performance that has been done without errors. In case of e=0, we can't use this equation because the division by 0 is not allowed. For that case the second part of formula is composed, which assigns productivity to usefulness. It means that if steganalysis method always performs without errors, all the work that is done will be useful.

The value reflects the usefulness during all the process of the steganalysis. To describe the method's usefulness in particular time, we should calculate productivity in given time period and use that value to calculate usefulness criterion value.

Unifying criteria

To summarize the results that are calculated using above given formulas and show them graphically, those criteria values have to be unified to one scale. For this reason the author defines special unifying formulas (*Table 1.*).

No.	Criterion	Unified value calculation formula (X – number of points)	
1.	Algorithms dependency (R)	$X \equiv R * 100/R_{max}$	(Rmax – maximal R value)
2.	Classification dependency (K)	$X \equiv K * 100/K_{max}$	(Kmax – maximal K value)
3.	Format dependency (G)	$X \equiv G * 100/G_{max}$	(Gmax – maximal G value)
4.	Accuracy (p)	$X \equiv p * 100/p_{max}$	(pmax – maximal p value)
5.	Error probability (e)	$X \equiv (100 - e) * 100/(100 - e_{min})$	(emin – minimal e value)
6.	Statistical detection level (l)	$X \equiv l * 100/l_{max}$	(lmax – maximal l value)
7.	Productivity (W)	$X \equiv W * 100/W_{max}$	(Wmax – maximal W value)
8.	Resource usage (C)	$X \equiv (100 - C) * 100/(100 - C_{min})$	(Cmin – minimal C value)
9.	Necessary information (B)	$X \equiv B * 100/B_{max}$	(Bmax – maximal B value)
10.	Usefulness (J)	$X \equiv J * 100/J_{max}$	(Jmax – maximal J value)

Table 1.   Unified value formulas

The unified formulas are based on the percentage equation. The largest value in each criterion is declared as the most effective one, not taking into account the error probability, because there the most effective is the minimal value. Maximal or minimal values of the calculated criteria are used in cases when the effective values are not defined in the task. When the effective values are found out, the percentage value for each criterion is calculated as proportion. If the effective value is the largest of all, it is calculated by formula (8), if the smallest (like in error probability), by formula (9).

$$\frac{X}{100} = \frac{V.}{V._{max}} \qquad (8)$$

where V – the value to be unified,

$V._{max}$ – maximal criterion value for given methods,

X – wanted unified percentage value.

$$\frac{X}{100} = \frac{100-V}{100-V_{min}} \qquad (9)$$

where V – the value to be unified,

V_{min} – minimal criterion value for given methods,

X – wanted unified percentage value.

Graphical representation

The main aim unifying the values is to reflect the values of the criteria graphically by using a diagram, as it is easier to evaluate efficiency of steganalysis methods and tools.

The author offers using the diagram that shows the unified values. The numbers of the criteria are shown on the x axis and the unified values in percents on the y axis of the diagram (*Figure 2.*).

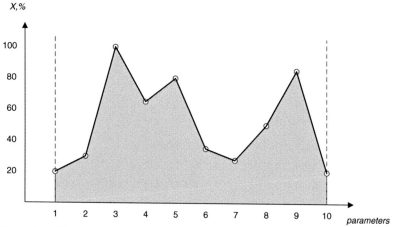

Figure 2. Citeria unified value diagram

By connecting the value points, we obtain the geometric figure that shows the efficiency of the steganalysis method or steganalysis tool (depending on the chosen evaluation object).

Obtaining every evaluation diagram gives the possibility to calculate the numeric value of the efficiency, which later can be compared to efficiency of other methods, and the most efficient steganalysis method can be chosen. The Efficiency value calculations are described in the next chapter (3.4).

Calculating the efficiency value

The author offers calculating the area of each method's diagram, for obtaining the efficiency value. The method which is described by the diagram of the largest area is considered to be the most efficient.

To calculate the area of the diagram, the efficiency picture should be transferred to coordinate axis. As the result we obtain the graphic of multiple linear functions (*Figure 3*). Transition from one criterion value to the other shows one of $y=f(x)$ linear functions. *Figure 3* shows the graphic that is split in to function areas. According to the mathematical rules, the area of the whole graphic is equal to the sum of the function areas.

Each area is calculated using the integral. So the final formula which calculates the total area of the diagram is as follows (10):

$$S = \sum_{i=1}^{N-1} \int_{if}^{i+1} (x)_i \qquad (10)$$

where N – number of criteria,

$f(x)$ – linear function in form of $y=kx+b$, where each function area is described; values for k and b are read from the graphic.

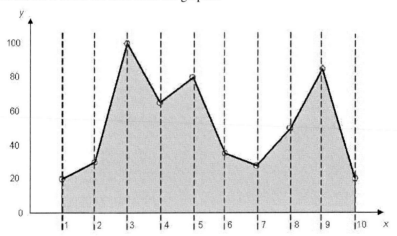

Figure 3.   Diagram which is split into function areas

As the result, every analyzed method has a calculated E ($E=S$ – efficiency value is equal to figure's area) value. Those values are compared and the method with the largest E value is supposed to be the most efficient. At this moment the process of evaluation and comparison is finished.

Proposing properties of the etalon method

No matter that work of evaluation system ends at the moment when the most efficient method or tool is found, steganalysis specialist can have a wish to find out, which method could be ideal for the particular case. This method is described by etalon model. The etalon model works inside particular problem, where the rules are previously set for that situation.

The author of the original research, on which this article is based, offers the solution for finding out the properties of this method. Based on the evaluation systems, there is a possibility to choose a maximal criterion method, which has all the criteria effective values. Next, using these properties, steganalytic has a possibility to elaborate the new steganalysis method with properties of the etalon method, or even better properties.

Practical SYstem ApPLication

As it was already mentioned, the elaborated evaluation system can be used both for analysis of the particular steganalysis methods and the steganalysis tools. The following task is defined for testing three chosen application programs to find the most efficient for graphic file steganalysis. There are 4 stego-media cover works available in JPEG, BMP, GIF and PNG formats.

Steganalysis software solutions are available on the Internet. This research doesn't create new software solution, that is why 3 programs will be examined in practice example. They are _StegSpy_, _StegDetect_ and _XstegSecret_.

Evaluation system says that comparison is done stepwise:
0   Defining the task.
* Calculating criteria values.
* Unifying criteria values.
* Diagram representation.
* Calculating efficiency values by using areas of the diagrams.
* Separating properties of etalon method (not compulsory).

The test situation is closely connected with the graphical file steganography because all the tools and methods described in this article are suitable for searching hidden information in graphical files. All the numeric results that are calculated during the comparison of methods are written in a table, so that they would be easier to comprehend (*Table 2*). Moreover, the last column in the table represents the efficiency value that is labelled with variable *E*.

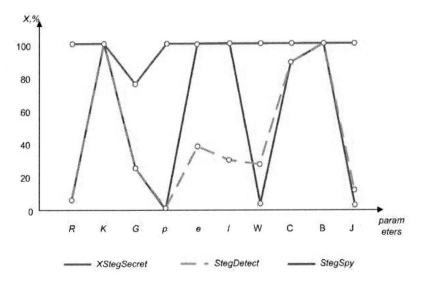

Figure 4. Obtained value diagrams

After calculating the criteria values and unifying them, the diagrams are obtained (*Figure 4.*). With the help of those, the most effective from three application products can be found. In this case it is easy to identify the most effective tool – XstegSecret, because almost all its diagrams' points are situated in maximal positions. Though, there could be situation when it won't be possible to diagnose efficiency using the diagram that is why it is always necessary to calculate value E using the method described before.

All the calculations are put in the result table (*Table 2.*) which clearly reflects all evaluation values.

Nr.	Value type	R	K	G	p	e	l	W	C	B	J	E
1.	cr. value	5	1	1	0	0	1	564	26	3	564	*505.9*
	u. value	7.4	25	100	0	100	100	2.2	90	100	2.2	
2.	cr. value	4	1	1	0	0.6	0.33	7197	28	3	2879	*239*
	u. value	5.9	25	100	0	40	33	28	88	100	11.25	
3.	cr. value	68	3	1	0.33	0	1	25588	18	3	25588	*875*
	u. value	100	75	100	100	100	100	100	100	100	100	

Table 2.   Fully completed efficiency table

CONCLUSION

The scientific article contains the description of the systematization of the steganalysis representation and its main problem. The problem is the difficulty to evaluate the efficiency of the used methods and tools in the particular situation.

As the result of this research, the system for evaluating the efficiency of steganalysis methods and software is introduced. This possibility is given by the set of criteria defined in the system. Methodology for calculating numeric value for each criterion is established. During the research an additional problem arose, which is the impossibility to combine criteria values, to put all the results in one set. To solve this problem the methodology for unifying criteria values is applied. Using unifying formula, it is possible to reflect the results as a diagram, as well as to calculate the area of the diagram, which is equal to efficiency value.

During the comparison of programs in the example situation, it is proved that the system, elaborated by the author, can be used in the real conditions. In the table of results the most efficient tool can be seen. The advantage of this system is its elasticity. The list of criteria can be adapted according to defined situation and rules. The disadvantage of applying this system is that it is time consuming. The reason is the variety of formulas and calculations for each method. This disadvantage can be solved by developing the appropriate software tool, with a help of which the evaluation system could work automatically. In the step of calculating the criteria values one more disadvantage exists – it is difficult to obtain parametres for some criteria. For example, while calculating the productivity, it was difficult to find out the time for steganalysis process execution. It wasn't possible to use debugger for this task that is why the value was measured with the help of the chronometer.

The research, described in this article, could be useful to steganalysis specialists and save their time spent for extraction process of hidden information and elaborating the new steganalysis methods.

Further, the following activities are planned:

1. Improving the calculations of the criteria numeric values.

2. Adding new criteria to the list.

3. Development of software for the evaluation system.

REFERENCES

Ingemar K. Cox, Matthew L. Miller, Jeffrey A. Bloom, Jessica Fridrich, Ton Kalker „Digital Watermarking and Steganography" // Burlington : Morgan Kaufmann Publishers , 2009 , p. 46-56, 469-494.

Yershov A., Rusakov P. "The Comparative Analysis of Digital Steganographical Methods LSB and Kutter" // The 46th Scientific Conference of Riga Technical University, Computer Science, Applied Computer Systems – October 13-14 – Riga, Latvia – 2005 – published in Scientific Proceedings of Riga Technical University, 5th series, Computer Science, Applied Computer Systems, Vol. 26, RTU Publishing, RTU – 2006 – pp. 186-197.

Eric Cole, Ronald D. Kruz „Steganography Art of Covert Communication" // Indianapolis: Wiley Publishing ,2003 ,361 lpp.

Andrew D. Ker „Benchmarking Steganalysis" Oxford University Computing Laboratory, UK //, In Chang-Tsun Li „Multimedia Forensics and Security" New York: Information Science Reference, 2008, p. 266-290.

Niel Johnson, Sushil Jajodia „Steganalysis: The Investigation of Hidden Information" // Center for Secure Information Systems, George Mason University, MS:4A4, Fairfax, Virginia 22030-4444, 1998, 4 lpp.

Gustavus J. Simmons „The prisoner's problem and the subliminal channel." // In D. Chaum, editor, Advances in Cryptology—CRYPTO 83, Plenum Press, 1983, p. 51–67.

Joshua Silman „Steganography and Steganalysis: An Overview" // August 2001, 8 lpp.

Joshua Michale Buchanan „MASTER DEGREE THESIS: Creating a robust form of steganography" , Wake Forest University, May 2004 – 99 lpp.

Fridrich J., Goljan M., Hogea D. „Steganalysis of JPEG Images:Breaking the F5 Algorithm." // Revised papers from the 5th International Workshop on Information Hiding. – October 2002. – 310-323 lpp.

AN INFORMATION SYSTEMS DESIGN THEORY FOR KNOWLEDGE MANAGEMENT SYSTEMS

Carlos Betancourt, Jan Aidemark

Växjö University, Växjö, Sweden

{cbeex07| jan.aidemark}@lnu.se

ABSTRACT

Knowledge has become one of the most important assets for companies nowdays. Knowledge Management (KM) uses organizational knowledge as a resource to make companies more competitive. Knowledge Management Systems (KMS) are gaining popularity, however, the failure rate remains high, with many projects not achieving their goals or being shut down early. KMS are often underestimated and treated as normal systems. IS practices do not cover certain aspects specific to KMS, aspects that do not show in other IS (e.g. socio-cultural issues). There are many studies concerning the KMS failures but they just focus on the symptoms and do not provide a solution to the problem. The goal of this master's dissertation is to generate a preventive tool that will help the KM field. With The experience gained by working in a real KMS project within a textile agency in Sweden and relevant literature, an Information Systems Design Theory (ISDT) for KMS was developed. As some authors suggest, KM needs an ISDT of it's own. An ISDT will guide practitioners through the process by restricting practices and features of the system to a more effective set. It will also encourage the academia to work on this theory for its improvement, completion, and validation.

INTRODUCTION

The effective development of new systems is an interesting topic for practitioners and researchers. An IS Design Theory's intention is to improve the development process. This paper proposes a new IS Design Theory for KMS, created in parallel with the project of B2C (Business-to-Customer) system for a Swedish textile agency.

Knowledge has become one of the most important resources (Little & Ray, 2005, p. 37; Jashapara, 2004, p. 8; Widén-Wulff, 2007) and the center of many companies' economy nowadays (Kluge, Stein, & Licht, 2002, p. 4; Jashapara, 2004, p. 9). Know how of the workers is the most important and valuable property that the enterprises have (Giddens, 1979, p. 69).

Despite the fact that there are many companies who have achieved high competitive advantages through the use of KMS (Bhatt, 2001), there is a high failure rate. Some researchers claim that the failure rate for KMS Projects is around 50 percent (Akhavan, Jafari, & Fathian, 2005). The audiences for this paper are KM specialists, researchers, practitioners, and in general people in the IT/IS field with an interest in KM. This ISDT is intended to improve the KM practices by reducing the failure rate. Analyzing relevant literature and working on a real case will be the base and means to get and prove our findings. An analysis of common mistakes and causes of failure will be the starting point in order to learn from the actual literature and to develop preventive measures. All the data and information collected from the action research inside the company was authorized for inclusion in this dissertation. The use of the Company Name and employees involved in the study was also authorized.

THEORETICAL BACKGROUND

Information Systems Design Theory (ISDT)

ISDT is a prescriptive theory whose purpose is the creation of paths that will help the production of effective IS based on theoretical foundations; it provides guidance to developers and is based on theory (Walls, Widmeyer, & El Sawy, 1992). An IS Design Theory will help the practitioners by limiting the features of the system and the development processes in order to improve the development process and achieve a higher success rates. An ISDT will tell, "how a design process can be carried out in a way which is both effective and feasible" (Walls, Widmeyer, & El Sawy, 1992, s. 37).

A Design Theory will help the developers, by letting them focus and limit their options and make the whole process more tractable, resulting in improved outcomes, and it will also suggest a hypothesis for the researches to test (Markus,

Majchrzak, & Gasser, 2002). The work of Markus et. al. (2002) served as a base, guide and example of the process and development that building a new ISDT implies.

Authors are more concerned in looking to the errors but not into stating procedures and principles for the better of the KM field (Bhatt, 2001). Literature on KM has not focused on why the KM initiatives fail and what can be learned from those failures (Little & Ray, 2005, p. 222), but merely on the sources of failure. The actual literature gives little or no theoretical guidance for designing and using requirements for KMS (Kakola, 2009). Knowledge Management is not as mature as other disciplines in the IS field, but it has reached the point where there is a need to develop a design theory of its own (Zilli, Damiani, Ceravolo, Corallo, & Elia, 2008). A better understanding of the design and use of KMS is still in an emerging state, both on the practice and academia (Walls, Widmeyer, & El Sawy, 1992, s. 37).

Unfortunately many projects have used the term KM to overprice their systems (Palmer, 2006). This issue has given a wrong reputation to KM of being just a fancy name for normal systems. Knowledge can be divided into individual and group knowledge and also into tacit and explicit. It is important to determine which knowledge is important and relevant and which knowledge is reified and marginalized (Hislop, 2005, p. 102). Dealing with the wrong knowledge will result in no benefits for the firm.

Common mistakes in KMS Projects

All Knowledge is codificable: Tacit knowledge is often wrongly defined as 'knowledge-not-yet-articulated' (Nonaka & Takeuchi, 1995), or knowledge waiting to be 'converted' or 'translated' to explicit knowledge (Little & Ray, 2005, p. 122). Tacit knowledge cannot always be codified into explicit knowledge, no matter how motivated the worker is, he cannot make explicit all his assumptions because he might not be even aware of all of them (Handy, 1984, p. 46). Converting tacit knowledge into explicit knowledge represents one of the major challenging tasks in KM (Nonaka, 1994). KM tools focus mainly on explicit knowledge, however it is important not to forget that effectiveness in firms is often achieved through tacit knowledge (Jashapara, 2004, p. 92). Explicit knowledge should not replace tacit, but complement and/or support it (Little & Ray, 2005, p. 342).

Lack of commitment from the managers: To get a better commitment from the top management a good understanding of their concerns is vital. As Jashapara (2004) refers to the Price Waterhouse Review (1995), the main concerns of the top managers in IT investment are: System is aligned with the organization's objectives, transformation through IT, infrastructure, uncertainty and budget. Keeping these concerns in mind along the entire project is good practice for gaining commitment from the top-executives. Commitment from the top managers is only at the initial state, when the system seems to be an add-on and easy task; once it gets complicated they draw back (Little & Ray, 2005, p. 223).

People willingness to share their knowledge: Another reason of partial or complete failure is the cultural and social factors (Handy, 1984, p. 41). Knowledge sharing is a complex process with infinite number of factors affecting the it (Widén-Wulff, 2007). Taking for granted that people will be willing to participate in knowledge management initiatives is a bad practice (Handy, 1984, p. 54). There are many reports that state people being reluctant to share their knowledge is not uncommon; motivation is a fundamental factor for knowledge sharing (Handy, 1984, pp. 44-45; Hislop, 2005).

KMS projects rely just on technology: One of the reasons of KMS failure is that projects rely merely on technology as their means for success. KMS projects do not often reach their expectations due to their high IT orientation (Jashapara, 2004, p. 129). As Bhatt (1998) mentions, KM is not just about technology. The interaction between technologies, people and techniques is what makes a KMS effective; this interaction is quite complex and specific for each organization, making it hard to copy from one place to another (Bhatt, 2001). Technology does not play the main role and should not be part of the core design, but it can surely impact the results of the project.

The cycle followed for this study is the one of Jashapara (2004) and for the development process, the ISDT was found in different literature (Avison & Fitzgerald, 2006; Harris, 1999; Friedman & Cornford, 1993).

Figure 1 Knowledge Management Cycle

METHODOLOGY

Type of Dissertation

This paper is a work-based dissertation at a master's level. The method followed was field research of KM, to learn more about the subject and to find out the common mistakes that lead projects into failure. Having all these theories, the next step was to do some research inside a company. Working within a real KMS project within a company will help test the theories and collect more information to build a Design Theory.

A qualitative method was chosen based on the research problem and its purpose. In this type of method skills and experience of the researcher impact the analysis of the data (Ghauri & Grønhaug, 2005, p. 110). The project data was collected using a qualitative research method.

Research Strategy

Kock (2005) among other authors states that for the IS, action research represents an important qualitative research method. Walls (1992) suggests action research as an appropriate research strategy for building design theories.

This research tries to make a difference in the KM field; therefore action research is an appropriate way of conducting this research. Action research makes it more convenient and easier by doing the study at the work place (Herr & Anderson, 2005, p. 2). It is a collaborative study between the researcher and the organization studied. Improvement of the KM theory is the desired outcome of this action research.

Herr and Anderson (2005), define action research as an investigation in an organization done by or with insiders. The collaboration between the insiders and the outsider (the researcher) will involve the researcher with important aspects and resources that need change (Herr & Anderson, 2005, p. 4) and that are relevant for the study. Knowledge will be created from problem solving in a real-life situation (Lewin, 1946). This means, using action research in a company to generate knowledge for the building of a design theory. Through action research, findings will be backed up, so they do not result in just unsupported generalizations, or as defined by Shaw (2003, p. 4) 'rules of thumb'.

Data Collection

Primary and Secondary data was used for this research. Interviews, emails and observation were the primary data sources. The data collection process started with the project description document created by Aldén & Olsson AB. Interviews and presentations to the staff and managers of the company were made in order to collect all the relevant data for the study.

ALDÉN & OLSSON AB: THE CASE

Introduction to the case

Aldén & Olsson AB is one of the biggest textile agencies in Sweden. Many of their products are manufactured in Asia, but their customers are located mostly in Scandinavia. The problem starts with the huge size of their design bank. The bank stores thousands of designs, and the rate of growth is quite high. Dealing with and managing all this expanding information is not an easy job. At the present time, the entire job is done manually, which means that they do not have a system for administrating and using the bank of designs. Printed catalogues and Windows Explorer are their current tools for searching different design patterns. Dealing with such a big quantity of information has an impact in the performance and quality of the services provided by the company and absorbs most of the available staff time in the Design Department, leaving no time for creativity and innovation (new designs creation) which is one of the main tasks of the department.

Different issues arise from these problems, which impacts the entire organization. The main problems/issues inside the company can be summarized as follows:

0   Information/Knowledge about the bank of designs and the customers preferences is limited to the memory of individual employees

- Knowledge is not in the organization, but in the employees
- Doing things manually takes longer time, affecting their service efficiency
- Design proposals for the customers are limited to what the staff can find or are aware of, not to what they have
- Creation of new designs does not take in to account the current bank of designs at all
- Designs are unorganized, uncategorized and often duplicated
- It is difficult to know if a design is available or if it was already sold
- Employees have almost no free time to create new designs

The design department is aware of the need for an IS to deal with the internal issues and improve both their work environment, and the quality of their services to the customers and the other departments inside the company. They are also aware that the knowledge resides only with employees and not in the organization; they see the need to become more knowledge oriented.

Company Processes/Activities

The different processes and activities in the Design Department are done manually and without the help of any system, apart from the Windows Explorer Search Tool, and the use of available printed catalogs. Relevant information for selecting the design patterns to present to the customer is held by the Sales Department, meaning that a constant exchange of information is done between departments every time a request is placed. This communication is done personally.

Another activity of the Design Department is the creation of new designs. The creation is influenced mainly by the new trends and the recommendations of the managers. The current bank of designs can influence the process but not as much as the other two factors just mentioned. The company offers both own designs and designs owned by suppliers.

System Features

It is important to point out that final proposition of the system is not the same as the first one defined by the Design Department. As the project progresses, adjustment and modification to the proposals are made. As the research learned more about the company and their problems, the solution took on different perspectives. However, the aim and objectives of the system remained the same throughout.

The Aldén & Olsson AB desired outcome is an improved service and relationship with their customers. This will be achieved by: a more efficient communication process with the customers, and the provision of a better service. This means offering the customer the best design patterns, chosen according to their specific needs and preferences. The basis for all this relies on the knowledge base, which will help the Design Department in the selection of the best design patterns according to each customer profile.

The system will have two interfaces: one for the staff in the Design Department and one for the customers. The former consists of a search engine, a statistics section and administration section. The search engine will include thumbnails in its search results. It will also have the option of narrowing the search results through the use of different parameters. Results can also be sorted by relevance, according to the particular preferences of individual customers. The statistics section will let the staff get different pictures about their bank of designs and the customer's database. They will be able to check which categories are selling more, which customers are buying more, which are the favorite suppliers, etc. The final section, administration, will let them add, remove, edit information about design patterns, customers, administrate the website profile section for each customer, etc.

The second interface is for the customers to access their profile online. This part of the system will let the clients place requests of design patterns according to their needs, check design patterns, previously authorized by the Design Department staff, and place the final order.

The prototype

The prototype had two main purposes:
- To show the company the results of the analysis and design phase. This will help them have a better picture of the system and its capabilities
- To learn and test results. Presenting the prototype generated, impressions, comments, as well as questions from the employees throughout the company. All these impressions were used in the analysis chapter. It also helped to test the system and to estimate the improvements that the KMS system will bring to the company.

Presenting a prototype, instead of a report was useful for the organization to visualize the system, avoid misunderstandings and enable them to give their comments, opinions and questions about it. The latter aspect was vital for the development of the IS Design Theory.

Improvements to the company

The system will improve the relationship with the customers and possibly later on the relationship with the suppliers. The use of a Customer Relationship Strategy will improve/build stronger relationship1s with clients based on mutual trust (Crosby, 2002), with this, the web interface will be the means of sharing more information with the customer, improving the relationship and improving the service timing. The system will generate knowledge that will help the staff in the Design Department to know better their customers and provide them better services. They will be able to know the preferences and characteristics of the customer, reducing their dependence on individual department members, who hold all the knowledge about the customers.

ANALYSIS

This chapter is the analysis of all the data collected from the work done together with Aldén & Olsson AB. The process followed, was of building up theories based on the literature research. As the process continued more vital information was collected, helping to build the theory. The project with the company served to test each of the theories found in the literature. During the whole process, different aspects identified in the literature arose. The action research made with the company complemented and contributed with valuable information that helped establish the ISDT.

Table 1 Initial ISDC and Problems Encountered While Attempting to Apply it *

Initial Requirements	Initial Design Theory	Problems Encountered when trying to apply the Initial Design Theory
Knowledge Management Design is a regular Information System Design	*The solution is a Knowledge Management System developed via SDLC*	
System Planning		
The organization is aware of the problem and defines a solution	Project will focus on the requirements stated by the organization	The solution proposed might not be the correct or optimal one
The organization decides to implement an Information System to solve their issues	Information System project is authorized by the executives	Executives ignore the roots and size of the problem
Planning of the project and optimal solution are proposed	Study concludes in the implementation of a Knowledge Management System	The organization might not be knowledge-intensive or prepared for a high-impact KMS implementation
System Analysis		
Different problems, issues and solutions arise after a system analysis (Knowledge-oriented)	List of requirements is reviewed and updated	Increased impact, work and socio-cultural issues are not contemplated
Codification of tacit knowledge into explicit knowledge	Processes are based on a knowledge-base	Replacing tacit knowledge and assuming a successful codification of knowledge
System Design		
Inputs, outputs, security, backup and processes of the system are defined	Design of the system (software and hardware)	Design does not keep in mind KMS issues and gets more technological

* Table structure for Table 1 and 2 was based on the work of Markus, Majchrzak, & Gasser (2002).

Table 1 shows how the problem was seen and handled at the early stages and the issues encountered. The first column represents the requirements and needs that arose as originally found. Following a normal IS procedure is represented in the second column, with the third column representing the problems found throughout the research process. After being aware of the problems, new requirements were defined to overcome these issues. These are represented in column one on Table 2. The second column is the first version of the guidelines that represent the principles of an IS Design Theory. These two Tables represent the process and problems found when doing the project within the company, as well as proposing how they should be addressed.

Table 2 Revised IS Design Theory for KMS *	
Revised Requirements	**Revised IS Design Theory**
Knowledge Management Design differs from SDLC	*The solution is a KMS, developed via its own methodology (Principles)*
System Planning	
• Original definition of the problem and the solution (by the organization) must not be taken as the optimal one. After analysis, different problems and solutions can be found	• The organization should be open for redefining and redirecting the course of the project towards a knowledge approach. This does not mean losing the alignment with the organization mission and goals but taking a knowledge orientation if needed
• Often users know better the roots and the reality of the problem and hold the knowledge in their minds while managers often have an unclear understanding of the problem.	• Workers should participate in the definition of the problem and shaping of the solution since the know better the roots of the problem and they also hold the organizational knowledge
• Organizations have different intensive-types. Not to take for granted that all organizations are knowledge-intensive or prepared to become knowledge-intensive	• Study must define organization's intensive-type and analyze the possibility and impact of becoming knowledge-intensive
System Analysis	
• Completing the requirements list is not enough. Different issues and challenges will arise through the process, managers are unaware of these problems	• Study the potential change and socio-cultural issues that might arise in further stages of the process • Management should be aware about these issues and agree to commit and continue the project
• Explicit knowledge can not replace tacit knowledge and transformation from tacit to explicit is not an easy task, not to mention that users might oppose to share their knowledge (if they aware it)	• Tacit and explicit knowledge are not exclusive; they complement each other. Users must be guided, motivated and rewarded to discover and share their knowledge
System Design	
• Project takes a technological direction, as the means for achieving success • Different phases of the development process focus on different aspects, forgetting or leaving behind the knowledge ones	• Choosing the best technological solution is not the main aim nor the strongest factor in the design • The design process should not lose its main aim which is managing knowledge at every stage

* Table structure for Table 1 and 2 was based on the work of Markus, Majchrzak, & Gasser (2002).

The following figure shows that all the different phases of the KMC should be present throughout the entire development process.

Figure 2 KMC and ISDC integrated model by the author (Principle #8)

Discussion

The result or outcome of this dissertation is the first stage in the construction of a IS Design Theory. This theory reflects the learning from all the process of this research. The different aspects learned from this research went through different stages. This dissertation should server both practitioners and researchers, people who are interested in the KM field as mentioned before. The research process within the study was really interesting, particularly in the way that is helped to evolve the definition of the problem. My picture of the problem and the solution evolved iteratively, providing a clearer validated picture as the different phases took place.

One of the most challenging issues of this research occurred at the early stages of the project. I was leaning more to the technical side, thinking basically as a computer science engineer (my bachelor's major), but after the advice and recommendations of my tutor, teachers, and opponents, I shifted more towards an IS direction.

Lessons Learned

From this research I learned many different things. Firstly, the fact that KMS might not be a completely new type of system. KMS do have special (developing) variables and require different skills. It is important not to underestimate this type of system, and prepare well for designing and developing them. It is better to start simpler and succeed, rather than stretching objectives that are over ambitious and bound to fail. Managers also need to not only provide support to the project, but also to commit to it. This demands their active participation and supervision throughout the project process. Another important aspect learned was how my picture of the problem and the solution evolved throughout the entire process. My initial approach to the problem and the approach adopted later in the research were very different, providing both, the study and myself and important outcome with valuable lessons.

CONCLUSIONS

As the result of this research, an IS Design Theory for KMS was created; it covers different aspects found in the literature and learnt through the case with A&O. The process was hard and it took quite some time, but the result makes all the work worth it. It is important to mention that the veracity and completion of this theory is still to be proven. This ISDT is intended to help practitioners and researcher to develop better practices when it comes to KMS. The intentions are that the theory can be taken as a guide for better practices and the basis for further research.

The ISDT is influenced by all the information found in the literature and by the project within the Aldén & Olsson Company. The result of using either data source in isolation would not have been the same. The combination of both helped to provide a better overall result and support for the project outcomes. It is important to emphasize the important role that the work of Markus et. al. played in this study. Their paper gave a better understanding of what an ISDT was and also a good example of the construction of this type of theory.

Based on the results obtained in this research and with the ISDT itself I can conclude that KMS indeed have special characteristics that demand a special treatment for a successful implementation. Having an ISDT represents a first step into many to take in order to learn more about KM and reduce the failure rates. This will let us focus on all the potential that KMS will provide in the future and forget about the common mistakes.

This intention of the tool is the improvement of the KM practices, although its effect and results depend totally on the user. If the user just makes a quick reading and does not follow the guidelines throughout the process, the impact of the tool will be practically none. This research represents a first version of an IS Design Theory for KMS. The ISDT created on this paper is to be improved and/or modified in the future by different researchers. Validation of the theory by other researchers is needed. It is important to emphasize that KMS projects should not rely entirely on the ISDT.

Figure 3 A proposal for Design Theory for Knowledge Management Systems

The figure contains the following text:

Characteristics of Knowledge Management Systems
(Kernel Theory)

Unforeseen problems/issues decrease management commitment
Different companies handle KMS an its impact differently
KMS do not mean 'state of the art' technology

Requirements for IT Support of KMS

KMS involve socio-cultural issues and a greater impact/change inside the organizations compared to other IS
KMS scope must be defined according to the organization's intensive-type
KMS must focus on other equally important aspects than just focusing on technology

KMS Support System Design and Development Principles

Include and evaluate KMS alternatives and re-define the project if needed
Users to participate in definition of problem and solution
Define organization's intensive type and knowledge management objectives
Define change, socio-cultural and impact issues in early stages
Confirm commitment and support from managers and users after studying and analyzing possible future issues
Develop good practices for enhancing, dealing, codifying and using knowledge
Technology as an important factor but not as the core for success
Design for Knowledge Management at every phase

Effective Knowledge Management System

REFERENCES

Akhavan, P., Jafari, M., & Fathian, M. (2005). Exploring Failure-Factors Of Implementing Knowledge Management Systems In Organizations. *Journal of Knowledge Management Practice* (85).

Avison, D., & Fitzgerald, G. (2006). *Information Systems development: Methodologies, techniques & tools* (4th Edition ed.). Maidenhead, Berkshire, England: McGraw Hill Education.

Bhatt, G. D. (2001). Knowledge management in organizations: examining the interaction between technologies, techniques, and people. *Journal of Knowledge Management , 5* (1), 68-75.

Bhatt, G. D. (1998). Managing knowledge through people. *Knowledge and Process Management , 5* (3), 165-171.

Bhatt, G. D. (2000). Organizing knowledge in the knowledge development cycle. *Journal of Knowledge Management , 4* (1), 15-26.

Crosby, L. A. (2002). Exploding some myths about customer relationship management. *Managing Service Quality , 12* (5), 271-277.

Davenport, T. H., & Laurence, P. (1998). *Working Knowledge: How Organizations manage what they now.* Boston, Massachusetts, USA: Harvard Business School Press.

Friedman, A. L., & Cornford, D. S. (1993). *Computer Systems Development: History, organization and implementation.* Chichester, West Sussex, England: John Wiley & Sons.

Ghauri, P., & Grønhaug, K. (2005). *Research Methods in Business Studies: A Practical Guide* (3th Edition ed.). Harlow, Essex, England: Pearson Education.

Giddens, A. (1979). *Central problems in social theory : action, structure and contradiction in social analysis.* London: Macmillan.

Handy, C. (1984). *The Future of Work: A Guide to a Changing Society.* Oxford: WileyBlackwell.

Harris, D. (1999). *Systems Analysis and Design: For the small enterprise* (2nd Edition ed.). Orlando, Florida, USA: The Dryden Press.

Herr, K., & Anderson, G. L. (2005). *The Action Research Dissertation: A guide for Students and Faculty.* Thousand Oaks, California, USA: Sage Publications, Inc.

Hislop, D. (2005). *Knowledge Management in Organizations: A Critical Introduction.* New York: Oxford University Press.

Jashapara, A. (2004). *Knowledge Management:: An Integrated Approach* (1st Edition ed.). Harlow, Essex, England: Pearson Education Limited.

Kemmis, S. (1982). *The Action Research Reader.* Geelong, Victoria, Australia: Deakin University Press.

Kluge, J., Stein, W., & Licht, T. (2002). *Knowledge Unplugged: The McKinsey & Company Global Survey on Knowledge Management.* Palgrave Macmillan.

Kock, N. (2007). *Information Systems Action Research: An Applied View of Emerging Concepts and Methods.* Laredo, Texas, USA: Springer.

Lewin, K. (1946). Action Research and minority problems. *Journal of Social Issues , 2* (4), 34-46.

Little, S., & Ray, T. (2005). *Managing Knowledge: An Essential Reader* (2nd Edition ed.). London, England: SAGE Publications.

Markus, L., Majchrzak, A., & Gasser, L. (2002). A Design Theory for Systems that Suppor Emergent Knowledge processes. (R. Zmud, Ed.) *MIS Quarterly , 26* (3), 179-212.

McDermott, R., & O'Dell, C. (2001). Overcoming cultural barriers to sharing knowledge. *Journal of Knowledge Management , 5* (1), 76-85.

Neef, D. (1999). Making the case of knowledge management: the bigger picture. *Management Decision , 37* (1), 72-78.

Nonaka, I. (1994). A Dynamic Theory of Organizational Knowledge Creation. *Organization Science , 5* (1), 14-37.

Nonaka, I., & Takeuchi, H. (1995). *The Knowledge-Creating Company: How Japanese Companies Create the Dynamics of Innovation.* New York, New York, USA: Oxford University Press.

O'Dell, C. (2000). *Stages of Implementation: A Guide for Your Journey to Knowledge Management Best Practice.* Houston, Texas, USA: American Productivity and Quality Centre.

Palmer, I. (2006, March 2). *Knowledge Management Failure.* (I. Palmer, Producer, & KDR Lab) Retrieved 03 3, 2009, from Oblique Angle: http://obliqueangle.blogspot.com/2006/03/knowledge-management-failure.html

Price Waterhouse. (1995). *Information Technology Review 1995/6*. London: Price Waterhouse.

Shaw, M. (2003). *What Makes Good Research in Software Engineering?* Carnegie Mellon University, School of Computer Science. Pittsburg: IEEE.

Walls, J. G., Widmeyer, R. G., & El Sawy, A. O. (1992). Building an information system design theory for vigilant EIS. *Information Systems Research , 3* (1), 36-59.

Widén-Wulff, G. (2007). *The Challenges of Knowledge Sharing in Practice*. Oxford, Great Britain: Chandos Publishing Limited.

Zilli, A., Damiani, E., Ceravolo, P., Corallo, A., & Elia, G. (2008). *Semantic Knowledge Management: An Ontology-Based Framework*. Lecce, Italy: Information Science Reference.

KNOWLEDGE TRANSFER IN ENTERPRISE RESOURCE PLANNING (ERP) PROJECTS: TOWARDS A FRAMEWORK FOR INCREASED LEARNING WHEN IMPLEMENTING ERP SYSTEMS

Erik Nilsson

School of Mathematics and Systems Engineering, Växjö University, Sweden

ABSTRACT

Companies spend considerable amounts of money on implementation of enterprise resource planning (ERP) systems. The implementation of an ERP system is risky since it involves the core administrative processes used to give a good customer service, plan and monitor production, handle suppliers and monitor the financial effectiveness of the company. It is quite clear that a wrongly managed ERP implementation can cause lower customer satisfaction and weakening trust from the market. These are effects that companies can't afford in most markets were competition is very strong and customer service is the key to future improved business. One very important part to minimize the risk in such projects is to focus on change management and knowledge transfer to the end users. The end users need to be equipped with the right knowledge in the new ERP system from day one, otherwise the risks grow considerable. Missing knowledge can cost missed deliveries, customer complaints, financial claims and most importantly lower compatibility on the market. This thesis builds a framework with main points to consider when building a positive learning environment and how to break the information wall so that the trainer can get through with the message.

Key words: ERP System, Cognitive theory, Change management, Learning

INTRODUCTION

Businesses all over the world are trying to leverage their IT investments in the best way. Information systems (IS) should provide all the necessary functions and information to the business and at the same time it should be cost effective. One type of information system is the ERP (Enterprise Resource Planning) systems that are implemented in most of the large enterprises in the world (Klaus, Rosemann & Gabel 2000). An ERP system assists enterprises in automating and integrating corporate cross-functions such as inventory control, procurement, distribution, finance, and project management (Tarn, Yen & Beaumont 2002). ERP systems have a number of packaged, predefined processes that are delivered with the system. These processes can to some extent be tailored to the specific needs that different companies have. To change the processes further than the ERP system supports is often very costly and is also working against the benefits of buying an ERP systems. Instead the organisations need to adopt their processes to fit the ERP system and the people in the organisation have to adapt to a change in their working environment (Tarn, Yen & Beaumont 2002).

It becomes a very delicate balance between the cost of IS investments and the benefits it gives to the receiving organisation (Tarn, Yen & Beaumont 2002). The way that the ERP system is implemented becomes crucial for how the organisation will benefit from it. It is natural that the persons affected by the changed ERP system are resistant to the change (Mento, Jones & Dirndorfer 2002). The challenge is to make the people in the organisation adapt to the new processes that the ERP system supports and to make them productive from day one (Soja 2006). An extra effort must be spent on the knowledge transfer process in order to avoid as much disruptions to the business as possible (Wang et al 2007).

As said before, implementation of a new ERP system will require the employees in the organisation to adopt their working process to the new system. Any employer in Sweden is required by the Swedish Work Environment Act to make sure that the work environment is designed in such a way that the employee is not subjected to physical or mental strains that can lead to ill-health(AML chapter 2:1). To put in place a new ERP system that, for some employees, is their only tool requires considerations to the changes in working environment. By informing and providing appropriate training to the employees, the risks of subjecting them to stress is reduced. It is therefore not only a business matter to work with the training and the change management when implementing ERP systems, it also in some way required by law to make sure that the employees are trained. Furthermore the Work Environment Act says that;

"The employee shall be given the opportunity of participating in the design of his own working situation and in processes of change and development affecting his own work" (AML Chapter 2:1)

The employee is therefore required to involve the personal in the changes to prepare them for the change and allowing them to participate in the design of their working processes. I would say that it gives an extra weight to the role of change management and end user training in ERP projects.

Current research exists in the areas of ERP implementation (Shtub 1999, Soh & Sia 2004, Scott 2005, Soja 2006, King and Burges 2006), change management (Fugate, Kinicki & Prussia 2008, Fedor, Caldwell & Herold 2006, Mento, Jones & Dirndorfer 2002) and cognitive psychology (Shuell 2001, Checkland & Holwell 1998, Wang et al 2007). These are of course very wide areas and there are a lot more references available than the listings above. At the moment there is no available research that combines knowledge from these different areas to show how the knowledge transfer process should be handled in ERP projects. I hope that in the future we will see more research done in this area and that the contribution that this thesis gives can be a starting point.

Purpose

This paper seeks to define a theoretical framework for knowledge transfer in ERP projects. Hopefully future research can follow and extend this framework to a methodology that can be applied in ERP projects to enhance the knowledge transfer process.

Knowledge transfer framework

To be able to get a deeper understanding of the subject I will make a journey through current research within three different fields that will build a framework for evaluation of the knowledge transfer process in one ERP implementation project. The first field is general research regarding ERP Implementations, mainly to get an understanding of what current research says about the methods to successfully implement ERP systems.

Next, it is important to study aspects of change management, mainly related to knowledge transfer to the end users in the organisation. And finally cognitive theory will be studied to get the knowledge on the current learning theories and research done. These three fields will then be combined to build a framework for knowledge transfer in ERP projects.

ERP implementation

Many factors influence the implementation of ERP systems. For large enterprises the most important factors are Pre-implementation analysis, financial budget and top management involvement. For small implementations; implementation experience and project management are the most important things (Soja 2006).

Another problem with the implementation of ERP system is the risk of misalignment between the ERP system and the organisation. The ERP system provides basic structures that are embedded in the system and these need to reflect the structures in the organization (Soh & Sia 2004).

Scott (2005) found that end user training is one of the top reasons for failing with the implementation of an ERP system. As many as 75 % of the respondents in his study reported that the next time they would spend more time on training and would tailor it more around their own business processes. Providing training too early or too late in the project, combined with the lack of tailoring compromises training effectiveness

Change management

The emotion highly influences the way that the employees are able to cope with organisational changes. Positive emotions give a higher degree of coping among the employees, and the other way around, negative emotions influence the coping negatively.

This would mean that if the organisation can positively influence employee's emotions in regards to an organisational change it would be possible to get a higher degree of coping which will affect the change positively (Fugate, Kinicki & Prussia 2008).

Each person will have their own frame of reference that will effect how resistant or open they are to the change taking place. Especially in the communication of the change it is important to look at the audience. People in the management team and the people affected by the change normally require a very different communication, which is reflected in their frame or reference. To open a dialog with the people most affected by the change can give important insight in their frame of reference and therefore make it possible to influence their acceptance towards the change (Mento, Jones & Dirndorfer 2002).

Cognitive psychology

Cognitive theories emphasise the acquisition of knowledge and the mental process rather than behaviour. Highly organised knowledge structures, rather than isolated facts, are seen as the outcome of learning. The focus is on understanding, problem solving and conceptual change rather than memorisation (Shuell 2001).

Traditional theories of learning view it as a stimulus-response framework. Basically it could be explained with a learner that responds to a stimulus in the environment, depending on what happens next (the occurrence of reinforcement or punishment), the probability that the learner will make the same response in the future either increases of decreases. These traditional theories focused on behavioural tasks rather than on adding components to the learner's cognitive structure. It is important to know that though these traditional theories didn't explain how individual come to understand complex ideas they provide a good understanding of why humans responds the way they do to a variety of stimuli and situations (Shuell 2001).

Knowledge about and ERP system must flow from those implementing the system to those responsible once in production. A fundamental component is that the learner has the capacity to receive the information from the knowledge holder. This capacity is called absorptive capacity. The learner's absorptive capacity is dependent on prior knowledge and experience within the particular field. It means that the organisations implementing ERP systems should build up their internal knowledge within the field in order to stimulate the knowledge flow during the project time line. Companies with greater internal knowledge will have a more successful ERP implementation (Wang et al 2007).

THEORETICAL FRAMEWORK

ERP implementation

There are many theories regarding the best way to implement an ERP system. It is important to get a background in what an ERP system is. It is particularly important to find out what characterises a successful ERP implementation.

ERP system

An enterprise resource planning (ERP) system is a system that completely or partly supports the core administrative processes across the company. The ERP systems are normally standard packages with a built in support for processes like finance, manufacturing, sales, distribution and human resources (Shtub 1999). Shtub also concludes that the ERP systems with their support of masses of different processes are hard to learn how to use and that it is hard to understand how to properly adopt the processes that the system offers. Many vendors offers ERP systems, the largest being the German software company SAP AG based in Walldorf. This company delivers an extensive ERP solution and also extensions such as portal solutions, supply chain management (SCM), customer resource management (CRM), development platform etc. According to SAP themselves quote

"Currently, more than 12 million users work each day with SAP solutions. There are now 121,000 installations worldwide, more than 1,500 SAP partners, over 25 industry specific business solutions, and more than 46,100 customers in 120 countries. SAP is the world's third-largest independent software vendor." SAP AG (2008).

At a fast reflection over the statement from SAP hits you that every day more people than the total Swedish population are working with this specific ERP system. Imagine now if we add the rest of the ERP vendors to this figure. It is very hard to estimate but a huge amount of people are daily managing their companies business using a standard ERP solution. It is very clear that this is a significant part of the administrative processes in the worlds companies that are managed using ERP software.

Problem with ERP implementations

One problem with the implementation of ERP system is the risk of misalignment between the ERP system and the organisation (Soh & Sia 2004). The ERP system provides basic structures that are embedded in the system and these need to reflect the structures in the organization. Soh & Sia (2004) says that an organisation implementing an ERP system should asses this misalignment prior to the selection of the ERP system and analyse its implication on a planned project. They found two types of misalignment; the first one is imposed misalignment, normally laws and government policies that companies have to apply to. The imposed misalignment where mostly surfaced at the 'as-is' or 'to-be' phases of the implementation, very late in the implementation. The organisation only adopted to the imposed structure misalignment in a few instances, instead the ERP system where modified to be able to handle the misalignment. The second type is voluntarily acquired misalignment, which where about management information, internal control, ease of use etc. In contrast these misalignments where to a majority managed by adoption of the organisation rather than modifying the ERP system. The implementation teams would explain the ERP process and information outputs, and propose various workarounds.

Soh & Sia (2004) found that the difficulty lies in the fact that the knowledge is distributed among several groups of people. Organisational members understand the laws they have to apply to and their industrial context well and the consultants understand the ERP system. The imposed structural misalignments often go unnoticed until very late in the project due to their embedded nature gives it a 'taken-for-granted' quality. It is therefore important to select consultants that have knowledge about the industry and the country.

Scott (2005) found that end user training is one of the top reasons for failing with the implementation of an ERP system. As many as 75 % of the respondents reported that the next time they would spend more time on training and would tailor it more around their own business processes. Providing training too early or too late in the project, combined with the lack of tailoring compromises training effectiveness. For users, learning the software is only one part of the training; relating it to their jobs is even more challenging. Scott (2005) found a number of points that are importing when writing the documentation about the ERP processes;

0   Documentation should focus on organization-specific business processes

- Role-based training would provide knowledge integration and better mapping to user needs.

- FAQs (frequently asked questions) should be available online.

Critical Success factors

The phrase critical success factors are used widely in the business by consultants and IT people to describe the key components of a successful implementation of an information system. These critical success factors are normally only a list of factors but provide little further guidance to those implementing the systems (King & Burges 2006). It is also hard to really know which factors really are the most important. Soja (2006) suggest that more research is needed to really understand what influences the factors, such as project scope, size of the project, budget and industry.

Soja (2006) did a thorough research regarding success factors in ERP implementations, which was based on the views of the participating people in the implementation. The study did not only find the success factors but where also able to see differences between success factors in large and small companies, between full scope and partial scope implementation projects.

It was found that the only considerable success factor for small business was the implementation experience of the consultants. For the large businesses this factor came last on the list of important factors. Instead, for large business, detailed schedule and top management awareness and involvement where significant success factors.

Large	Small
Detailed schedule	Implementation experience
Top management awareness	

Large	Small
System reliability	
Implementation goals	

Table 1: Success factors depending on company size (Soja 2006)

For full scope projects the most important success factors where system reliability and the project team. On the other hand for the projects with partial implementation scope it was most important with financial budget and top management support.

Full implementation scope	Partial implementation scope
System Reliability	Financial Budget
Project team Empowerment	Top Management Support
Team composition	Investment plan
Linking with company strategy	Detailed schedule
	IF infrastructure
	Team involvement

Table 2: Success factors depending on scope of project (Soja 2006)

Soja (2006) concludes that the wider the implementation project, i.e. the longer its duration and the larger the enterprise, the greater influence on the project success has the definition of detailed schedule and setting the implementation goals. Also for the case of extensive projects, one has to pay special attention to the reliability of the system introduced.

King and Burges (2006) dig's beyond the critical success factors and argues that we should explore social capital theory and social exchange theory to be able to explain;

- *Why* top management support ERP projects
- *Why* project champions promote the ERP implementation. Project champions are explained as key users or representatives from the organisations that devote their time to the ERP implementation.
- *Why* department users might support or resist the change.

Social capital is the value of the networks in the organisation, "capital is seen as a social asset by virtue of actor's connections and access to resources in the network or group of which they are members" (Lin 2001). King and Burges (2006) uses the theory of social capital to stress the importance of building relationship in the organisation between all the three organisational parts of an ERP implementation; top management, project champions and the department users. They mean that these organisational units must build a network that shares the same ideas to enable a successful implementation. If part of these networks gets unbalanced, there could be implications for the implementation, for example if the relationship between top manages and the departmental users are historically bad, or if the support of the project champions (person appointed by the Top management to lead the ERP implementation) have been bought by promoting them. They also add a cognitive aspect by saying that the project champions might perhaps go naïve through close and regular contact with the vendor staff and therefore get too used to the vendors language and the superiority of the new system so that they lose the close bond with the department users. The outcome of the imbalance in the relationship between the three parts of the organisation described above could lead to a high social capital in the relationship between top management and the champions, high social capital between champions and the vendors but low social capital between top management and department users and also low social capital between the project organisation and the department staff.

Social exchange theory works much alike economical exchange. Social exchange assumes that individuals take part in an exchange only when they expect their rewards from it to justify the cost of taking part in it (Gefen & Ridings 2002 see King and Burges 2006). Gefen and Ridings (2002) continue to describe an experiment that showed that when the project team responded to the end users demands rapidly and positively, the end users also provided greater support ("approval") to the project. A positive social exchange between all the different groups will in turn deliver a higher social capital and a positive effect on the project.

I believe that we will get much more understanding of the factors influencing the success of implementation projects if we study the social capital and social exchange theories instead of studying lists of critical success factors. Good relation ship and respect between people in the organisation is necessary to be able to build a dynamic and well working organisation. It is important to motivate the different types of people that take part in an organisational change or system implementation, direct (project team) or indirect (end users), so that that all feel that there will be a benefit from a positive participation.

CONCLUSION

The theoretical framework presented in this paper shows that correct communication between management and employees, between the project and the end users, between the end user participating in the project and those who are not, are very important. By letting people know what is happening in the project it creates a good learning environment, which has been shown to be very important. The response from the employees interviewed showed that they who where involved in the project where more positive to the change, compared to those who didn't get as much information. The negative attitude towards the project affected their interest in learning and affected their capabilities to understand the new processes. It is clear that any ERP project should think much about the way that they are communicating with the end users. The extra effort taken to manage this communication will be paid back in increased performance from the employees and a positive atmosphere in the project. My experience is that implementation of an ERP system always requires changes in the processes, affecting the end users the most. And at the end, when the ERP system is in place, the success of the implementation depends on how well these end users can manage their work in the new system. The focus must be to give them the right foundation by training them to do their job using the new ERP system. Theories presented in the thesis shows that building a positive learning environment, by creating a balanced social capital and positive social exchange (King & Burges 2006), and by increase coping (Fugate, Kinicki & Prussia 2008) and create higher employee commitment (Fedor, Caldwell & Herold 2006), gives a great reward in the ability that employees will accept the changes. These theories form the first part of the framework which focuses on creating a positive learning environment.

Final discussion

I think that this thesis gives enough motivation to any ERP implementation project to focus greatly on the change management and the training during the implementation. An ERP project is a great deal more that finding solutions to technical problems. It is a change that effects the employees in the organisation and this change need to be managed in a proper way. I suggest that one role in an ERP project should be responsible for coordination of the change management related activities. This role should have the responsibility to manage the way the change is brought to the organisation. It includes;

- the organisation of the project in terms of involvement from the business. The business always has to contribute with resources and it is important that these resources have the competence required by this role. The case study earlier in this thesis showed how wrong it can get when the wrong person takes on this role. It is important that the responsible persons from the business are coached in their way to integrate and include their colleagues in the project. The aim is to keep a balanced social capital and positive social exchange within the organisation.

- the management of the communication throughout the project. By regularly communicating project status, decisions, achievements etc to all people affected by the change. The communication doesn't necessarily need to be done by the change management responsible but it should be controlled and structured by this role. The aim is to increase the acceptance to the project and increase the employee's ability to cope.

- the design of the training strategy. By building a common concept for how the training to the end users should be designed. The different types of employees needs should be taken into account by building their ability to learn during the project, so that their absorptive capacity is increased. It is also important to establishing a common vocabulary that everyone understands, both trainer and student, so that the training can be conducted in an efficient way.

It should be of the interest for businesses implementing ERP systems to invest in such a role as the one described above. But I realize that it requires knowledge and understanding of the importance to focus on change management. To my experience the training and communication to the people around the project always have a lower priority than the design and the implementation of the processes in the system. All the ERP implementation projects that I have been part of had a very tight time line and it is easy to cut in the area of change management. I guess that part of the reason is the limited knowledge in the effects that change management has on the end result of a project. While the managers of ERP implementation often are very skilled in the implementation of the ERP system they have less knowledge in the softer parts related to change management that I have described in this thesis.

Future research

This thesis focused only on the knowledge transfer process in ERP projects. The result became very much a contribution to change management since I realised that the training phase of the project is not independent of the other parts of the project. To build a good environment for learning you need to focus on this from the start of the project. It would be interesting to dig deeper into this and to understand how current change management theories can benefit from what has been learnt in this thesis. It would also be interesting to know if the findings in this thesis could be adopted in other types of IT projects as well, maybe even in projects that are not directly IT related.

REFERENCES

Boynton, A C.; Zmud, W.; Jacobs, G C. (1994). The Influence of IT Management Practice on IT Use in Large Organizations. *MIS Quarterly*. Vol 18. No 3

Checkland, P and Holwell, S. (1998). *Information, Systems and Information Systems*. Sussex: John Wiley & Sons, Ltd.

Dierickx, I, Cool, K (1989). Asset stock accumulation and sustainability of competitive advantage. *Management Science*. Vol 35 No 12.

Eriksson, D, M (2007). Phenomeno-semantic complexity: A proposal for an alternative notion of complexity as a foundation for the management of complexity in human affaris. E:CO Issue. Vol 9 pp 11 – 21.

Eriksson, D, M (2007). Phenomeno-semantic complexity: A proposal for an alternative notion of complexity as a foundation for the management of complexity in human affaris. E:CO Issue. Vol 9 pp 11 – 21. Quotes Ogden, C.K. And Richards, I.A. (1985) The Meaning of Meaning: A Study of the influence of Language upon Thought and the Science of Symbolism, ISBN 9780744800333

Fedor, D, B, Caldwell, S, Herold, D, M (2006). The effects of organizational changes on employee commitment: A multilevel investigation. *Personnel psychology.* Vol 59, pp 1 – 29.

Fugate, M, Kinicki, A, J, Prussia, G, E (2008). Employee coping with organizational change: and examination of alternative theoretical perspectives and models. *Personnel Psychology.* Vol 61, pp 1-36

Glaserfeld, Ernst von (1995), Radical constructivism, A way of Knowing and Learning, Antony Rowe Ltd, Eastbourne.

Gomm, R, Hammersley, M, Foster, P. (2000). *Case study method.* London: SAGE Puplications Ltd.

Hart C (2005) *Doing Your Masters Dissertation.* London: SAGE Puplications Ltd.

Johnson, P. (2003). *Understanding Management Research : An Introduction to Epistemology.* London: Sage Publications, Incorporated.

King, S F, Burges, T F. (2006). Beyond critical success fators: A dynamic model of enterprise system innovation. *International Journal of Information Management.* Vol 26 pp 59-69.

King, S F, Burges, T F. (2006). Beyond critical success fators: A dynamic model of enterprise system innovation. *International Journal of Information Management.* Vol 26 pp 59-69. Quotes;

Gefen, D., & Ridings, C. M. (2002). *Implementing team responsiveness and user evaluation of customer realationship management: A quasi-experimentaql design study of social exchange theory.* Journal of Management Information Systems, 19(1), pp 47-69

Klaus, H, Rosemann, M and Gabel G (2000). What is ERP. *Information Systems Frontiers.* Vol 2:2 pp 141-162

Lin, Nan (2001). *Social Capital : A Theory of Social Structure & Action.* Port Chester, NY, USA: Cambridge University Press

Mento, A J, Jones, R M, Dirndorfer, W (2002). A change management process: Grounded in both theory and practice. *Journal of Change Management.* Vol 3, No 3.

Merriam, S B. (1998). *Qualitative research and case study applications in education.* San Francisco : Jossey-Bass

Rockmore, T. (2005). *On constructivist epistemology.* Maryland: Rowman & Littlefield publishers, Inc.

Royce, W W. (1970). *Managing the Development of Large Software Systems: Concepts and Techniques.* Technical Papers of Western Electronic Show and Convention (WesCon) August 25-28, 1970

Scott, J E (2005) Post-implementation usability of ERP training manuals: the user's perspective. *Information systems management*, Spring 2005.

Shtub, A. (1999). *Enterprise Resource Planning (ERP). The Dynamics of Operations Management.* New York: Kluwer Academic Publishers.

Shuell T.J. (2001). *Learning Theories and Educational Paradigms.* Elsevier Science Ltd.

Shuell T.J. (1996) *Teaching and learning in a classroom context.* In Berliner D.C, Calfee R.C *Handbook of Educational Psychology.* Simon and Schuster Macmillian. 1996, pp. 726 – 764.

Soh C, Sia S K (2004). An institutional perspective on sources of ERP package-organisation misalignments. *Journal of Strategic Information Systems.* Vol 13, pp 375 – 397.

Soja P. (2006). Success factors in ERP systems implementations: Lessons from practice. *Journal of Enterprise Information Management.* Vol 19 No.4 pp 418-433.

Tarn, M J, Yen D C and Beaumont M (2002) Exploring the rationales for ERP and SCM integration. *Industial Management & Data Systems.* Vol 1 pp 26 – 34.

Thurén, T. (2007). *Vetenskapsteori för nybörjare.* Malmö: Lieber AB.

Wang, E T G, Lin, C C-L, Jiang, J J, Klein, G (2007) Improving enterprise resource planning (ERP) fit to organizational process through knowledge transfer. . *International Journal of Information Management.* Vol 27 pp 200 – 212.

Yin, R. K (2003). *Case Study Research, Design and Methods,* 3rd ed. Newbury Park, Sage Publications.

SAP AG (2008). *SAP History: From Start-Up Software Vendor to Global Market Leader.* Accessible at http://www.sap.com/about/company/history.epx . (24/03/08)

REDESIGN OF A LOAN DISBURSEMENT PROCESS USING BUSINESS PROCESS SIMULATION – A CASE STUDY FROM A MAJOR GERMAN BANK

Sabrina Arndt, Maximilian Hollmann, Michael Leyer

Frankfurt School of Finance & Management, Sonnemannstraße 9-11, 60314 Frankfurt am Main, Germany

{ sabrina.arndt | maximilian.hollmann | m.leyer }@ fs-students.de

ABSTRACT

Simulation is often used in process redesign projects, but within banks this does not hold true. Therefore, this paper presents an example how business process simulation (BPS) can be used within the banking context. As a sample the loan disbursement process of a major German bank was chosen for redesign. The main problem of the process was that cycle times were too high and employees did not work process-oriented. Furthermore, the relationship managers had major problems to fulfil their primary task of contacting customers. The support of BPS enabled the development and evaluation of two promising redesign possibilities. Surprisingly the introduction of a workflow system did not lead to the best results. Simple and cheaper methods like a relocation of processes shortened the cycle time and had a greater impact on the reduction of transaction costs while additionally disburdening the relationship managers.

Key words: Business Process Simulation, Business Process Redesign, Banking, Case Study

INTRODUCTION

Based on the ideas of Hammer & Champy (1993), manufacturing companies were the first to replace their traditional functional business structures and implemented a process driven view. Starting in the mid-nineties with a few companies of the service sector, today the banking industry is slowly adopting process thinking as well. Especially with regard to the rapidly changing financial services industry, bank managers are forced to concentrate on business processes. In this context various instruments exist, but the depth of the multifaceted possibilities and benefits which come along with the process view are not fully utilized yet (Heckl & Moormann 2010).

Especially the loan business, the cornerstone of traditional banking services, faces an increasing competition. In order to gain scale advantages and to be in a position to offer lower-cost loans, industry members continuously analyze opportunities for improving the business processes. Here, the introduction of process management techniques in combination with workflow management systems seems to be promising. For this case study, a transaction process within the retail-banking division of a major German bank was chosen. The loan disbursement is processed in several departments of the bank. It covers the loan disbursement of a mortgage which starts after the loan agreement is finished. The process is initiated when the client wishes a full or partly payout of the loan amount, e.g. to pay a callable real estate purchasing price or to settle payable invoices for a building under construction. Main problems are that employees are not working process-oriented and therefore the cycle times are too high. Additionally, the relationship managers have not enough time to take care of their customers due to several administrative tasks. For this process a redesign supported by business process simulation (BPS) of a loan disbursement is conducted. The aims of the case study are to reduce the cycle time and the transaction costs per disbursement.

Chapter 2 gives an overview of the basic theoretical foundations of BPS in the context of business process redesign. Based on this, the redesign of the loan disbursement process is described in chapter 3. This is done by following typical steps for a simulation project. Chapter 4 summarises the results and gives an outlook on further applications of BPS for redesign projects in the banking industry.

BUSINESS PROCESS SIMULATION IN THE CONTEXT OF BUSINESS PROCESS REDESIGN

In the literature a business process is referred to as a logical sequence of steps with a defined beginning and end, in which employees and machines are creating an output (Scheer 1998; Rosenkranz 2006). Moreover, a business process is repeatable, produces an additional value and is not limited to a specific unit or function. Zarei (2001, p. 1327) defines business processes as "a set of logically interconnected activities through which actors convert inputs into outputs to achieve a certain purpose".

Due to continuously changing environmental conditions the ongoing adaption of business processes is a decisive factor for the agile organisation. In order to achieve this goal, a strict management of business processes is essential (Davenport & Short 1990). The proliferation and widespread attention being paid to business change paradigms, such as business process reengineering, has created a market for organizational techniques. Fundamental changes caused by a process redesign may cause unforeseen problems and shortcomings which need to be corrected. This led to the widespread analysis of business processes using techniques such as flow charts, process maps and simulation software. Here, BPS has emerged as a prominent application to prevent the emergence of failures within a redesign project (Cheung & Bal 1998).

Simulation enables understanding the foundations of business processes, generating opportunities for change, and assessing the effects of those changes (Doomun & Jungum 2008). As Paul & Giaglis & Hlupic (1999, p.1552) point out „complex (process) design decisions may affect different, but interacting and interrelated dimensions of an organization: its processes, its people, its strategy, its environment, its culture, its information policies, to name but a few". A change in any of these aspects may result in unexpected consequences for the others. Simulation modelling is a way to evaluate these consequences before implementation without having to test them in the real-world setting (Neumann & Rosemann & Schwegmann 2008).

The advantages of using upfront simulations of potential could-be processes are multifaceted. Most important of all "simulation replaces the wasteful and often unreliable practice of setting management policies based on trial-and-error methods" (Verma & Gibbs & Gilgan 2000, p. 55). This is mainly due to the circumstance that conducting a simulation before the existing process is actually changed, eliminates the risk of unforeseen cost inefficiencies, under-/ overutilization of resources, bottlenecks or the incapability of a process to meet regulatory requirements. As Law & Kelton (2000) stress, simulation allows managers to evaluate multiple process designs and perform "what-if" types of analyses. Moreover "the ability of BPS to incorporate system variability makes it a useful technique to provide a realistic assessment of the need for and results of change" (Greasley 2003, p. 419). Ultimately, Paul et al. (1999) argue that BPS even helps to justify the costs for changes and allows comparing the merits of design alternatives.

But, there are also limitations of BPS. Most importantly one has to keep in mind, that there is no algorithm behind the conduction of a simulation. It is rather a tool to acquire knowledge and reach some informed decisions regarding a real-world system (the business) – which is majorly supported by and dependant on human intuition (Paul et al. 1999). Beyond that Peppard & Rowland (1995) are wary of the use of simulation analysis in the redesign of processes because of the potential time and cost which are required to build simulation models. In this context Robinson (1994) highlights that the estimation of the amount of resources required should be limited according to the study objectives. Most important of all though is that BPS is limited in a sense that it can only be used to check the efficiency of process design ideas and that it does not replace the development of innovative process architectures (Greasley 2003).

Despite these limitations, BPS is widely regarded as an effective tool to support redesign projects. Today there are various simulation programs available (e.g. Arena, iGrafx, etc.) which provide a user-friendly format. Within this case study the simulation tool iGrafx is used.

CASE STUDY: REDESIGN OF A LOAN DISBURSEMENT PROCESS

In the following, the typical steps for conducting a simulation study within a redesigning project are applied as shown in Figure 1.

Step 1	Step 2	Step 3	Step 4	Step 5
identifying goals, primary objectives and scope of the project	gathering data on the existing process	building, validating and implementing a model of the current process	performing what-if analysis by making changes to the model and running simulations	presenting results and recommendations for potential changes to the current process

Figure 1: Steps for conducting the simulation (following Lee & Eclan 1996)

Modelling the as-is process

The goal of reducing cycle time and average process costs was identified as the primary objective of the case study (Step 1). The scope of the project was determined to focus exclusively on the disbursement process starting with the customer disbursement order and finishing with the external payment to a third party, e.g. a real estate vendor or a property developer. Based on this, data of the existing process was gathered by the authors' expert opinion and observational research (Step 2).

Following the data collection, a simulation model was built using the simulation software iGrafx (Step 3). A process map was constructed which shows the main activities – indicated by rectangle shapes – and decision points – indicated by diamond shapes (Figure 2). The single icons are connected by arrows to display the logic of the process. In addition to the process logic enclosed in the process map, the simulation requires further data in order to enable a dynamic analysis of the system, in contrast to a static model which is mostly illustrated by a flowchart-type process map (Greasley 2003).

To ensure this, the activities were filled with process data such as the number of workers which is required to perform a certain task or the duration of the single activities which was modelled assuming normal distributions of estimated times. Each decision point contains a probability for a yes/no option.

The process map is divided into three swim lanes: "Client" for the customer, "Relationship Management (RM)" for the customer adviser and "Credit Factory" for the back office.

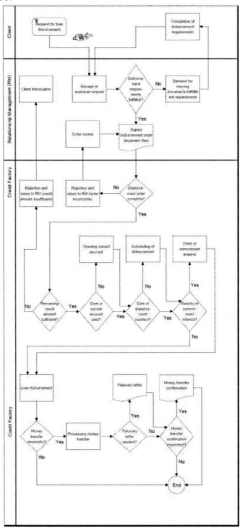

Figure 2: As-is process diagram of the loan disbursement process

The software iGrafx contains a generator which can initiate customer requests in a certain time schedule according to the observations in practice (iGrafx 2009). In the model of the loan disbursement process, the generator triggers customer requests for a simulation period of 36 months according to a time-table starting at 8 am and ending at 6 pm with a certain distribution of transactions that authentically replicates the occurrence of real-life requests. Against this background the current process was outlined as follows:

Starting point is the request for a loan disbursement that normally reaches the bank by call, but may also come up by letter or fax. The relationship manager receives the request and checks whether the disbursement requirements are fulfilled. These requirements typically consist of the contract-compliant constitution of collaterals that have been agreed on in the mortgage contract. Generally this is the notarized charge on land or, as the case may be, other collaterals like life insurances or fixed deposits. Furthermore the mortgage contract may impose conditions that have to be fulfilled before the first disbursement, e.g. to present a proof of equity or an original income statement that has been missed during the credit check. If the disbursement requirements are not fulfilled, the relationship manager informs the client who then has to take care of the completion of the disbursement requirements. If the requirements are fulfilled, the relationship manager signs a disbursement order which contains all relevant information like the beneficiary of payment and the construction progress of the building and sends the document via fax to the credit factory.

In the credit factory a dispatcher checks whether the disbursement order is complete and signed by an employee possessing credit approval competency according to the requested amount. If that is not the case, the dispatcher rejects the order and sends it back to the relationship management to make an order review. Otherwise a team of workers in the credit factory executes the further processing of the order which starts with a check whether the (residual) amount of the loan is sufficient for the requested disbursement. If that is not the case, the order is rejected and sent back to the relationship manager, who then has to inform client. Afterwards another check is performed in order to verify whether the client already has a current account which is necessary for the booking of disbursement and further payment to a third party. In a few number of cases, a new current account has to be opened. The next decision covers the question of maturity dates. Some disbursement orders are not due at this point in time and therefore have to be rescheduled to a future date. Each mortgage contract offers a time of two months which are free of commitment interest. If the client makes disbursements later, the commitment interest is charged accordingly.

The following step is the loan disbursement which consists of crediting the requested amount of money on the client's current account. In most cases a money transfer to a third party has to be made which is instructed to pay on the disbursement order document. Otherwise the process ends. In case a money transfer is needed, the worker in the credit factory has to check whether it is necessary to send a fiduciary letter to the bank of the beneficiary. This is the case if the collateral is transferred by matching the payment with the delivery of collateral. As a final aspect it has to be checked whether the client requested a money transfer confirmation. After the sending of this confirmation is initiated, the process ends.

Before the model results are analyzed, the model behaviour was checked to ensure that the model is providing valid results for the purposes of the simulation study (Greasley 2003). Therefore the model builders performed a structured walkthrough of the model, test runs and check of the animation display. The times of each single activity as well as the overall times were compared to the real-world system.

Analysis of the as-is process and potential opportunities for improvement

Once the model was validated, it was run over a simulation time period of 36 months and the results were tracked according to the project focus on cycle time and average costs. The following tables show an excerpt of the time and cost reports.

Count	Avg Cycle	Avg Work	Avg Wait	Avg Res Wait	Avg Block	Avg Inact	Avg Serv
9738	279	51	228	5,4	1,8	220,8	58,2

Table 1: Overall transaction times (minutes)

The average cycle time of all 9.738 simulated disbursement requests that have completed the as-is process during the set time period was recorded to be 279 minutes. It can be devided in an avarage work time of 51 minutes and an avarage waiting time of 228 minutes. Here, work time means the amount of time during which work was actively being performed on transactions and is calculated from activity task duration times. Waiting time describes the amount of time that transactions spend waiting, which consist of inactive, blocked and resource wait time. The detailed report shows a breakdown of avarage cyle times and work times of each swim lane.

	Count	Avg Cycle	Avg Work	Avg Wait	Avg Res Wait	Avg Block	Avg Inact	Avg Serv
Client	9738	0,00	0,00	0,00	0,00	0,00	0,00	0,00
Credit Factory	9738	100,2	20,4	79,2	<0,6	0,00	79,2	20,4
Relationship Management	9738	178,8	30	148,8	5,4	1,8	141	37,8

Table 2: Transaction times divided by swim lanes (minutes)

The cycle times of the customer swim lane are set to zero per definition, because the goal of the process study was to measure the cycle time of a disbursement transaction inside the bank. The time the client needs, e.g. for the notary appointment, may not be directly influenced by the bank and therefore it is not coverd by this redesigning project. Most interesting is the split-up of cyle time between the credit factory (100,2 minutes) and relationship management (178,8 minutes). In the input data assumtions, the relationship managers spent an estimated 40% of their working time attending appointments with clients, so the waiting time for the disbursement process is rather high. When the relationship managers are out of office, they cannot work on administrative tasks. As the disbursement is an administrative task it is suboptimal that the high-salaried relationship managers spend more time on the process (30 minutes) than the workers in the credit factory (20,4 minutes). In a potential to-be process this relation should be the other way around in order to release the relationship managers from administrative work and set time free for client related sales tasks.

The waiting times of average 148,8 minutes in the relationship management department can be identified as a bottleneck of the process and should be improved by balancing the work load passing through the process towards the credit factory.

Count	Avg Cost	Avg Lbr Cost	Avg Eq Cost	Avg Oth Cost	Avg Std Cost	Avg OT Cost
9738	31,86 €	30,48 €	0,00 €	1,39 €	31,86 €	0,00 €

Table 3: Overall transaction costs

Regarding the number of disbursement orders that have been simulated, the avarage costs (costs accumulated by transactions, including resource costs and any other fixed costs) are Euro 31,86 per disbursement process. The labour costs are the most important cost driver representing 95.7% of the average costs. The remaining 4.3% are variable costs which occur along the process.

Since most of the work of the relationship managers is performed manually, the processing speed is relatively low which leads to delays. The customer advisors, paid by high hourly rates, have to fill in documents for disbursement, send faxes to the credit factory and spend time on administrative tasks instead of doing their core tasks consisting of sales and distribution. For a large amount of time they are currently occupied with administrative jobs which may also be done by workers who are paid at lower hourly rates. The goal for redesigning the process should be to reduce the workload resulting from administrative tasks of the relationship managers. Thus one road of improvement could be a relocation of activities from relationship management to the credit factory, where hourly rates and thus labour costs are lower (could-be process 1). This would set some time of the relationship managers free which they can use to take care of their customers and spend more time selling banking products.

Another potential road of improvement could be an automated processing of certain steps in a workflow system replacing some of the manually performed activities (could-be process 2). This redesigning opportunity may reduce labour costs by utilization of non-human resources.

In the next chapter, what-if analyses are performed by making changes to the model according to the potential directions for improvement and simulations are run to compare the process performances (Step 4). Afterwards the results of these could-be processes are presented and recommendations for changes to the current process are given (Step 5).

Could-be process 1: Relocation of process steps into the credit factory

The idea behind the first potential alternative process is to disburden the relationship managers. Therefore, the process steps should be restructured and simultaneously the majority of steps – especially the time consuming ones – relocated into the credit factory. Figure 3 shows how the restructuring and relocation influence the process design and the sequence of process steps.

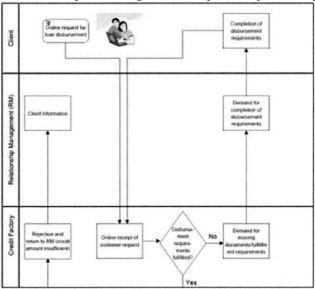

Figure 3: Relocation of process steps into the credit factory

The customers' requests for loan disbursement in this case can only be done online by the client himself and therefore arrive in the company in a digital form. These online requests are directly received by the credit factory. There the workers of the credit factory check whether the disbursement requirements are fulfilled. If that is the case, the further process remains the same as it is in the existing as-is process like presented in chapter 3.1. If the disbursement requirements are not fulfilled, and only then, the relationship manager is called who then has to inform the customer and ask for the completion of the documents.

Could-be process 2: Introduction of a workflow management system

Besides the idea of relocating process steps into the credit factory, there was another idea for a redesign and potential upgrade of the loan disbursement process developed. As the current loan disbursement process is very labour-intensive for the relationship managers – which drives the cost for the completion for each loan disbursement to a high level – the process as it currently exists is not competitive. Therefore the replacement of the current process with an automated workflow management process was modelled in iGrafx to understand the potential new approach of loan disbursement (Figure 4).

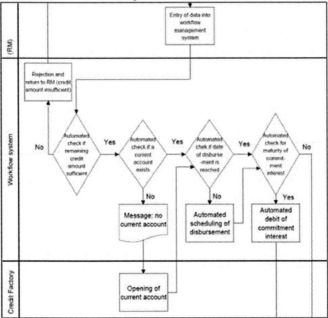

Figure 4: Introduction of a workflow management system

The introduction of a workflow management system influences the process design and the   sequence of process steps fundamentally. The new aspect about this second could-be process is that the relationship manager – after checking if the disbursement requirements for the customers' disbursement request are complete – enters the data concerning the loan disbursement into a workflow management system (visualized in the process diagram by introducing a fourth swim lane "Workflow System"). It is estimated that this step takes between five and ten minutes. The following steps which concern the remaining credit amount, the existence of a current account, the date of disbursement and the maturity of the commitment interest are then automatically processed by the workflow system. As long as all requirements for the disbursement are fulfilled and no extra steps like the opening of a current account, etc. are needed, the disbursement order runs through all the process steps automatically and finally debits the commitment interest. If the workflow system finds the check for the sufficiency of remaining credit amount to be negative, the system self-actively rejects the disbursement and sends a message to the relationship manager. In case the system discovers that the client does not have a current account yet, it automatically sends a message to the credit factory, so that the credit factory employees can open one. If the workflow system finds that the date for disbursement is not reached yet, it self-actively schedules it to the correct disbursement date. After the automated debit of commitment interest, the employees of the credit factory take care of the execution of the loan disbursement and the potentially following steps concerning money transfer, fiduciary letter and money transfer confirmation as described in the introduction of the as-is process (Chapter 3.1).

Simulation results and redesigning recommendations

The simulation models which were developed provide valuable knowledge about cycle time and transaction costs as well as a better understanding of the relationship between single process parameters (process steps).

Table 4 shows that both could-be processes have the ability to reduce the average cycle time considerably, by roughly 30 minutes and 60 minutes respectively. The monetary amount per loan disbursement is for the current process on average Euro 31.86. The relocation of process steps into the credit factory as simulated in could-be process 1, resulted in a cost reduction of more than 50%. This is primarily due to the reduction of average labour costs. With the introduction of a workflow system the costs can only be reduced by 24%.

	As-is Process	Could-be process 1	Could-be process 2
Average cycle time	279	234,6	213
Average cost	€ 31.86	€ 15.41	€ 24.27

Table 4: Comparison of cycle time (minutes) and transaction costs

As presented, the results of the simulation allow predicting process performance along a number of measures like cycle time and costs. Looking at these measures alone it becomes obvious that both alterative process redesigns are an improvement to the existing process. Before giving a recommendation as to whether the implementation of one of the potential processes makes sense – and if so which process redesign is most promising – the soft factors like customer satisfaction, which remain disregarded in the modelling and simulation, need to be considered (Schmelzer & Sesselmann 2002).

For the could-be process 1 the savings of cycle time as well as costs (primarily due to a reduction of labour costs resulting from the fact that credit factory workers are less expensive than relationship managers) are tremendous. However, it is important to be aware that, as customers are not given one single contact person any longer, as it was in the case with the relationship managers in the existing loan disbursement process, the process redesign is attended by a simultaneous effect which might be perceived by clients as a limitation of customer friendliness.

For the could-be process 2 the impact of change was – regarding average cycle time and average work time – larger than for could-be process 1. The average costs however remained at a higher level due to the running costs of the workflow management system. Another driver for the overall costs, which is not considered in the simulation yet, is the necessary upfront acquisition of the workflow system, which needs to be surcharged on the simulation results.

Furthermore, a detailed analysis of the allocation of the work time (Table 5) shows that only could-be process 1 disburdens the relationship managers effectively. In this case, they would have more time for the acquisition and support of customers. This could lead to an increasing number of sales potentially facilitating a higher earning for the bank.

	As-is Process	Could-be process 1	Could-be process 2
Average work time Relationship Manager	30	13,2	29,4
Average work time Credit Factory	20,4	43,2	12

Table 5: Comparison of work time (minutes)

CONCLUSION

BPS is used seldom in the banking industry for the redesign of processes. Nonetheless, this paper has pointed out, that BPS is an effective tool to analyse and redesign business processes in banks. It allows to evaluate the as-is process and to conduct experiments with potential changes before they are implemented. Doing this, it supports change decisions without disrupting any existing operations.

Within this case study, the example of a loan disbursement process within a major German bank was chosen. Having analysed the actual process, the result was the identification of a bottleneck within the relationship management department. This is caused by a wrong allocation of tasks within the existing process. To solve this problem, two possibilities for the reduction of administrative workload of the relationship managers were developed.

The results of the simulation of the two possibilities show that they both have a positive influence on the overall cycle time and transaction costs, although to a different extend. Concerning the cycle time could-be process 1 is worse, but halves the transaction costs. On the contrary, could-be process 2 is better in terms of reducing the cycle time, but transaction costs are cut only by one third. Furthermore, only could-be process 1 reduces the administrative workload per disbursement of the relationship managers. Since this allows them to spend more time on sales, one might recommend could-be process 1 based on the simulation results.

However, for complex processes it is impossible to include all features of the real system in the simulation model (Verma et al. 2000). Despite the valuable quantitative information concerning the two possible redesigns, the results of the simulation study have to be assessed carefully. Before one decides for the final redesign, qualitative aspects should be considered. This could be for example an analysis whether customers are willing to use an online disbursement application.

REFERENCES

Cheung, Y. and Bal, J. (1998), "Process analysis techniques and tools for business improvements" in *Business Process Management Journal*, 4 (4), 274-290.

Davenport, T.H. and Short, J.E. (1990), "The New Industrial Engineering. Information Technology and Business Process Redesign" in *Sloan Management Review*, 31 (4), 11-27.

Doomun, R. and Jungum, N.V. (2008), "Business process modelling, simulation and reengineering: Call centres" in *Business Process Management Journal*, 14 (6), 838-848.

Greasley, A. (2003), "Using business-process simulation within a business-process reengineering approach" in *Business Process Management Journal*, 9 (4), 408-420.

Hammer, M. and Champy, J. (1993), "Reengineering the corporation: A manifesto for business revolution", Harper Collins, New York.

Heckl, D. and Moormann, J. (2010), "Operational Process Management in the Financial Services Industry" in *Handbook of Research on Complex Dynamic Process Management: Techniques for Adaptability in Turbulent Environments* (Wang, M. and Sun, Z. Eds.), pp. 529-550, IGI Global, Hershey/PA.

iGrafx (2009), "Rapid Learning Guide", http://www.igrafx.com/downloads/documents/iGrafx_Rapid_ Learning_Guide_09.pdf [Access: 24.08.2009].

Law, A.M. and Kelton, W.D. (2000), "Simulation Modeling and Analysis", 3rd Edition, McGraw-Hill, New-York.

Lee, Y. and Eclan, A. (1996), "Simulation Modeling for Process Reengineering in the Telecommunications Industry" in *Interfaces*, 26 (3), 1-9.

Neumann, S., Rosemann, M., and Schwegmann, A. (2008), "Simulation von Geschäftsprozessen" in *Prozessmanagement. Ein Leitfaden zur prozessorientierten Organisationsgestaltung* (Becker, J., Kugeler, M., and Rosemann, M. Eds.), pp. 435-453, 6th Edition, Springer, Berlin.

Paul, R.J., Giaglis, G.M., and Hlupic, V. (1999), "Simulation of Business Processes" in *American Behavioral Scientist*, 42 (10), 1551-1576.

Peppard, J. and Rowland, P. (1995), "The Essence of Business Process Re-engineering", Prentice Hall, Hempstead.

Robinson, S. (1994), "Simulation projects: building the right conceptual model" in *Industrial Engineering*, 26 (9), 34-36.

Rosenkranz, F. (2006), "Geschäftsprozesse, Modell- und computergestützte Planung", 2nd Edition, Springer, Berlin.

Scheer, A.W. (1998), "ARIS – Modellierungsmethoden, Metamodelle, Anwendungen", 3rd Edition, Springer, Berlin.

Schmelzer, H.J. and Sesselmann, W. (2002), "Geschäftsprozessmanagement in der Praxis: Kunden zufrieden stellen – Produktivität steigern – Wert erhöhen", 2nd Edition, Hanser, München.

Verma, R., Gibbs, G.D., and Gilgan, R.J. (2000), "Redesign check-processing operations using animated computer simulation" in *Business Process Management Journal*, 6 (1), 54-64.

Zarei, B. (2001), "Simulation for Business Process Re-Engineering: Case Study of a Database Management System" in *Journal of the Operational Research Society*, 52 (12), 1327-133

Editors

Dr. Markus Helfert is a lecturer in Information Systems at the School of Computing, Dublin City University (Ireland). He obtained a PhD degree in Information Management from the University of St. Gallen, Switzerland, a Master Degree in Business Informatics from the University Mannheim, Germany and a BSc in Computing and Business from Napier University – Edinburgh, Scotland. His research is centred on Information Quality Management and includes research areas such as Data Warehousing, Healthcare Information Systems, Supply Chain Management and Information System Architectures. He is programme chair for the European Master of Science in Business Informatics.

E-mail: Markus.Helfert@computing.dcu.ie

Mouzhi Ge is a research scientist at the Technical University of Dortmund in Germany. Meanwhile he is also affiliated at the Dublin City University in Ireland as a senior researcher. His research interests are mainly focused on information quality management, information system modelling and recommender systems.

E-mail: Mouzhi.Ge@tu-dortmund.de

Howard Duncan is a lecturer at the School of Computing, Dublin City University (Ireland). His research interests are in Business Process Management, Software Engineering and Project Management. He teaches courses in Business Organisation, Application Programming and Business Process Management.

E-mail: Howard.Duncan@computing.dcu.ie